YOKO ONO
ARIAS AND OBJECTS

BY
BARBARA HASKELL
JOHN G. HANHARDT

BOOK DESIGN   MATTHEW YOKOBOSKY

PEREGRINE SMITH BOOKS SALT LAKE CITY

This is a Peregrine Smith Book, published by
Gibbs Smith, Publisher
P.O. Box 667
Layton, Utah 84041

Manufactured in Singapore

Cover photographs:
Front: from *Yoko at Indica* (exhibition brochure), 1966; photo by Iain Macmillian
Back: filmstrip from *No. 4* (also known as *Bottoms*), 1966

Photographs copyright as noted in the accompanying captions. All photographs not specifically credited are the property of the Lenono Photo Archive. All rights are reserved.

Library of Congress Cataloging-in-Publication Data
Haskell, Barbara.
    Yoko Ono, arias, and objects / Barbara Haskell and John Hanhardt.
      p. cm.
    ISBN 0-87905-386-0 (pbk.)
    1. Ono, Yōko—Criticism and interpretation.   I. Hanhardt, John G.
II. Title.
NX512.056h37 1991
700'.92—dc20   91-2304
                                                                CIP

First edition
94 93 92 91   6 5 4 3 2 1

Texts on Yoko Ono copyright © 1991 by Barbara Haskell and John G. Hanhardt
Texts by Yoko Ono copyright © Yoko Ono
All songs copyright © Ono Music except:
"Air Talk," "Angela," "Have You Seen a Horizon Lately ," "Now or Never," "Sisters, O Sisters," "Song for John," "Sunday Bloody Sunday," "We're All Water," and "Woman is the Nigger of the World" copyright © Ono Music Ltd.
"Every Man Has a Woman Who Loves Him," "Kiss Kiss Kiss," and "Walking on Thin Ice" copyright © Lenono Music.

All rights reserved. No part of this book may be reproduced in any manner whatsoever without written permission from the copyright proprietor, except for brief quotations used for the purpose of review.

INTRODUCTION
by   Barbara Haskell and John G. Hanhardt

CONSTRUCTS AND CONCEPTS
by   Barbara Haskell
with commentary on film and video by John G. Hanhardt

Instruction Pieces	14
Nature: Flux and Transformation	22
Early Performance Works	28
London Exhibitions: 1966 and 1967	40
Music of the Mind	48
Linguistic Paradox	54
Sky and Clouds	62
Camouflage	70
Paintings to Complete in the Mind	77
Equivalence	81
Flying	84
Feminism: Violence and Liberation	90
Body Innocence	98
Political Activism	106
Evocations of Love	114
Vanguard Vocals	122
Mourning	128
Bronze Age	134

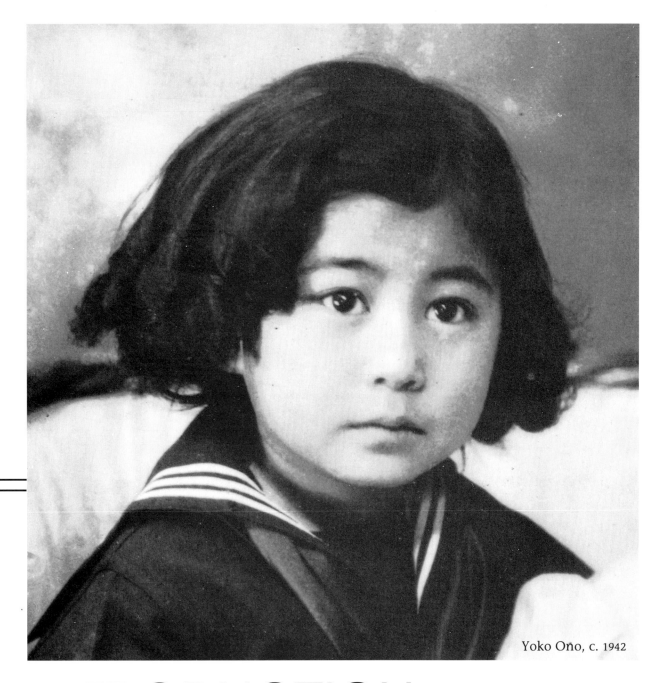

Yoko Ono, c. 1942

INTRODUCTION

Yoko Ono's association with John Lennon after 1968 instantly tranformed her into an icon of popular culture. Ironically, this fame obscured rather than enhanced the legitimacy of her independent achievements as an artist. In fact, her success as a performance artist, object-maker, singer, songwriter, filmmaker, and author preceded her relationship with Lennon and has continued after his death. In an artistic career whose accomplishments have too often been overshadowed by the glare of superstardom, Yoko Ono created an important and provocative body of work which uniquely fused the radical innovations of the aesthetic vanguard with a distinctly Oriental sensitivity.

Yoko Ono entered the avant-garde art world in the crucial period of the early 1960s. She joined a generation of artists who challenged traditional forms of art and questioned previously held definitions of artistic expression. Chafing at what they viewed as the limitations imposed on art by their elders, a number of dancers, painters, sculptors, musicians, poets, and filmmakers banded together to challenge aesthetic boundaries; the overlapping and interpenetration of art forms gained supremacy.

Yoko Ono, c. 1943   Yoko Ono, c. 1944

Out of this new interdisciplinary spirit arose a non-narrative form of theater which initially found expression in what were known as happenings. Extolling the concept of "total art," happenings implicitly challenged the traditional separation between media. Why, artists asked, should they limit themselves to painting and sculpture? Why should musicians and composers work only in sound? Attracted by the idea of extending painting into actual space and time, a group of experimentally minded younger artists amalgamated action, sound, light, and movement with gesturally conceived tableaux. The results resembled fast-action surrealist plays, in which non-actors engaged in a series of compartmentalized events whose constituent actions were self-contained and consequently nonlinear. Instead of the traditional theatrical emphasis on character and narrative, the focus in happenings was on props, costumes, and sets. That these items were primarily constructed out of cast-off urban materials intentionally countered the notion of art as something separate from life.

This direct incorporation of concrete, scavenged aspects of the everyday world was partially inspired by the work of John Cage, who believed that the boundaries between art and life should be eliminated. For Cage, the world itself was a work of art; he saw the aesthetic potential in the commonplace and accepted everyday noise as music. Making music was, therefore, a means of revealing to people the beauty around them. It was, as he wrote, "an affirmation of life—not an attempt to bring order out of chaos nor to suggest improvements in creation, but simply a way of waking up to the very life we're living, which is so excellent once one gets one's mind and one's desires out of its way and lets it act of its own accord."

By means of chance and audience participation, Cage was able to literally incorporate the sounds and activities of life into his art. In performing Cage's 1952 composition *4'33"*, pianist David Tudor came out onstage, lifted the lid of the keyboard, and sat at the piano, without playing, for the duration of the piece—exactly 4 minutes and 33 seconds. The random sounds and unexpected visual events that happened within the time span constituted the work of art. By thus insisting that the audience provide the "music," Cage had conflated the roles of the audience and performer.

Visual artists since the turn of the century had incorporated found objects into their compositions. But Cage's performance went much further in removing traces of the artist's personal control from the making of art. Even Marcel Duchamp, with his ready-mades, had not so overtly challenged the definition of what constituted artistic authorship. Cage's embrace of chance and his belief in the viability of nontraditional sources of aesthetic material redefined the function and meaning of art. These lessons were not lost on the generation of artists who emerged in the 1960s.

Indeed, the unmediated presentation of tangible and everyday subject matter linked the various arts—from the direct presentation of images from popular culture in pop art to the use of "real" time in film and the deployment of commonplace movement in dance. Incorporating images, sounds, and movements that did not overtly rely on the artist's expressive gesture offered an exit from what artists viewed as mannered stylization and self-conscious emotionality in the art of their predecessors. The very act of presenting commonplace subject matter, without any evidence of artistic manipulation, posed a severe challenge to notions of artistic originality and the function of art. Yet the new art did not abandon subjectivity and meaning so much as transfer it to the viewer, who was thus forced into a more decisive role in determining the content of art.

These theoretical constructs engendered another mode of performance art, parallel with happenings, which drew its inspiration from Cage's embrace of chance and his expansive attitude toward musical material. Identified with the Fluxus group—a loose affiliation of avant-garde musicians, visual artists, and poets—this new form of performance took the assault on traditional definitions of art one step further than had any previous art form. Drawing on the legacy of Surrealist and Dadaist soirées of the early decades of the century, Fluxus artists often reduced their Events, as some termed their performances, to unitary gestures enacted in unadorned settings by performers wearing ordinary street clothes. As with vanguard dancers who likewise incorporated commonplace, task-oriented activities into their vocabulary, many Fluxus artists favored a conceptual rigor and attentiveness to "insignificant" phenomena: a light going on and off, or a line of performers shuffling across the floor. Typically, a deadpan wit pervaded the disciplined enactment of these isolated, quotidian actions. In Alison Knowles' *Proposition* (1962), performers came out onstage, made a salad, and exited; Emmett Williams' *Voice Piece for La Monte Young* (1963) instructed the performer to ask whether La Monte Young was in the audience, and then leave. Because of the focus on single-gesture actions, this type of Fluxus Event was easily expressed as written performance instructions. Sometimes these took the form of aphoristic poems: La Monte Young's *Composition 1960 #5* instructed performers "to release a butterfly or any number of butterflies into the air"; George Brecht's *String Quartet* consisted of the words "shaking hands." As poetic stimulates to viewers' imaginations, these cryptic phrases were equally valid as performance directives or states of mind; although they could be enacted, simply reading and thinking about them was sufficient to constitute realization.

Fascinated by the aesthetic potential of this new form of expression, Yoko Ono became an active and early participant in the vanguard activities associated with Fluxus. Indeed, one of the seminal events which launched Fluxus was a concert series, organized by La Monte Young, which Ono hosted at her loft at 112 Chambers Street. Presented from December 1960 to June 1961, the "Chambers Street Series," as it was informally dubbed, offered one of the first collective forums for the avant-garde sensibilities that later emerged under the rubric Fluxus.

As with other of her colleagues, Ono's aesthetic expressions amalgamated visual phenomena, movement, and sound. Her first public concert took place at the Village Gate, New York, in 1961, as part of an evening of three contemporary Japanese composers. Among Ono's contributions was *A Grapefruit in the World of Park*, a multimedia mélange which included a tape of mumbled words and wild laughter, musicians playing atonal music, and a performer intoning unemotionally about peeling a grapefruit, squeezing lemons, and counting the hairs on a dead child. In *Toilet Piece*, which drew on theories of chance and audience participation, she amplified the sounds made in the lavatory; in *Clock Piece*, she placed a clock on the center of the stage and asked the audience to wait until the alarm went off.

Later in 1961, Ono had an evening of performance events at Carnegie Recital Hall, the first in an impressive list of concerts she gave through 1968. Many of these incorporated the matter-of-fact, task-oriented activities which had become a virtual trademark of the vanguard performance community. Featured in the program were *A Grapefruit in the World of Park, A.O.S.*, and *A Piece for Strawberries and Violins*. In the latter work, a performer stood up and sat down before a table stacked with dishes. At the end of ten minutes, she smashed the mound of dishes. Her action was accompanied by a rhythmic background of repeated syllables, a tape recording of moans and words spoken backwards, and an aria of high-pitched wails sung by Ono—a portent of the musical sound that would later become Ono's trademark.

Detail of poster from Ono's concert at Carnegie Recital Hall, 1961.

A distinguishing feature of Ono's performance work was her desire to intensify viewers' internal awareness and introspective meditation. She facilitated a state of dreaming by paring down visual and auditory stimuli and by concentrating thought on a single idea or isolated perception. "The natural state of life and mind is complexity," she wrote in 1966; "...what art can offer...is an absence of complexity, a vacuum through which you are led to a state of complete relaxation of mind. After that you may return to the complexity of life again." Ono's desire to highlight the stillness of the self by engendering a focused concentration drew on the tradition of Zen meditation practice. Emulating Zen methods, she aimed to free viewers of the mind's clutter in order to effect a clarity of perception. Accordingly, *A.O.S.* was performed in the dark, in total silence; the only audible sound was the noise produced inadvertently in the process of enacting the performance. She hoped, in this way, to jolt her audience out of habitual patterns of listening and thinking. "If my music seems to require physical silence," she stated, "that is because it requires concentration to yourself—and this requires inner silence which may lead to outer silence as well. I think of my music more as a [Zen] practice (gyo) than as music. The only sound that exists to me is the sound of my mind. My works are only to induce music of the mind in people."

Central to Ono's work was her attention to the intangible forces of nature: in *Wind Piece* (1962), the audience was asked to move their chairs to make a narrow aisle for the wind to pass through; in *Sun Piece* (1962), she instructed them to "watch the sun until it becomes square." Typically restricted to short phrases, these events resembled Zen Buddhist koans, whose paradoxical quality was intended to stimulate poetic reveries—as in *Tape Piece I* (1963), whose instructions were to "Take the sound of the stone aging," and *Cloud Piece* (1963), which admonished the participants to "imagine the clouds dripping. Dig a hole in your garden to put them in."

Yet Ono's performance work was not limited to mystical evocations of ineffable phenomena. Implicit in much of her work was a subversive attack on conventional notions of morality and violence. In *Cut Piece* (1964), Ono sat impassively on stage while members of the audience came forward and cut off pieces of her clothes until she was nearly naked; in *Wall Piece for Orchestra* (1962), she knelt on the stage and repeatedly hit her head against the floor. Pervading these works were proto-feminist questions about the nature of personal violation and violence, which found later expression in *Rape* (1969), a cinematic exposition on the victimization of women.

In the spring of 1961, Ono began a group of paintings and objects which paralleled her performances in their subject matter and their dependence on chance and audience participation. In these instruction pieces, as she dubbed them, Ono extended her expansive attitude toward musical sound to mutable visual phenomena by providing the structure of the work—the canvas—but not its specific visual material, which was left to the discretion of the audience. These works were conceived initially as written performance scripts: the instructions for *Painting to Be Stepped On* were to "leave a piece of canvas or finished painting on the floor or in the street." Eventually, Ono translated these performance scripts into two- and three-dimensional objects. But she did so without forfeiting the reliance on audience participation and, by extension, chance. *Painting to Be Stepped On* became an actual piece of canvas, lying on the floor, waiting for the surface markings that would occur when viewers stepped on it. Likewise, *Painting to Hammer a Nail* became a white board with a hammer attached to it, ready to receive the nails that the audience was encouraged to pound into its surface.

As conjunctions of object and performance, these works were not static, discrete objects; instead, they embodied notions of becoming and metamorphosis. Like her Events, they exuded a profound respect for organic transformation. In contrast to other "nature artists," Ono did not freeze one single moment from an organic continuum, but incorporated the actual process of metamorphosis into her pieces—as in *Smoke Painting* (1961), whose instructions were to light a canvas with a cigarette and observe the ensuing smoke, or *Painting for the Wind* (1961), whose structure allowed the wind to disperse seeds around the world.

As with her performance scripts and music, Ono's objects and paintings eliminated visual distractions in an attempt to focus viewers' concentration. *Painting to See a Room Through* (1961) was a canvas with a tiny, almost invisible hole in its center that one peered through to see the room; *Painting to See the Skies* (1961) contained two holes in the canvas through which viewers could see the sky.

Some of these pieces were intended to be completed only in the mind. *Painting to Be Constructed in Your Head* (1962) called for viewers to observe three paintings carefully and then to mix them well in their heads. *Part Painting* (1961) instructed viewers to rearrange mentally, in any way they desired, the various pieces of a painting that Ono had scattered around the room. Her goal in transferring realization exclusively to the imagination was to further the viewers' sense of wonderment and extend their creative potential—to "allow them to release their inhibitions and allow their own rather nebulous thoughts a freedom of expression."

Ono with *Painting[s] to Hammer a Nail*, 1970.

In July 1961, Ono exhibited a selection of these early works at the AG Gallery on Madison Avenue, which George Maciunas had opened the previous fall with fellow Lithuanian emigré Almus Salcius. Maciunas closed the gallery several months later and moved temporarily to Europe, where he tirelessly worked to organize concerts and publish multiples of the work of Japanese, American, and European artists who were linked under the name of Fluxus. A staunch supporter of Ono's work throughout his life, Maciunas forged the official link between Ono and Fluxus.

Apart from her exhibition at the AG Gallery, Ono's public activities concentrated primarily on conceptual and performance events until 1966. In September of that year she was invited to participate in the "Destruction in Art Symposium," a conference of artists from around the world which was held in London. She remained in the city following the symposium, staging performances and film showings and arranging gallery shows in two of London's most highly respected vanguard venues: the newly opened Indica Gallery and the Lisson Gallery. Her presence on the London art scene was sufficient to earn her the epithet "the High Priestess of the Happening" and caused one reviewer to remark that she seemed as ubiquitous in the city as Stilton cheese and Princess Margaret.

Ono's Indica Gallery exhibition, in November 1966, included a new group of audience-participation pieces as well as work whose union of text and object resembled a three-dimensional version of an aphoristic poem. *Pointedness* (1964)—whose text reads, "This sphere will be a sharp point when it gets to the far corners of the room in your mind"—resonates with the perplexing obscurity of a Zen construct. Likewise, the glass keys in *Keys to Open the Skies* exist less as physical objects than as springboards for poetic ruminations about a world beyond the rational one of time and space. Ono's reversal of normative assumptions of reality in order to provoke new perceptions finds its counterpart in her linguistic conundrums. *Three Spoons* (1967) confounded verbal common sense by presenting four spoons, while the sign *This Is Not Here* (1966) did the same by patently denying verifiable reality.

By 1967, when Ono's "Half-a-Wind Show" opened at the Lisson Gallery, she had unleashed her poetic speculations about the nature of reality. Her inclusion in this exhibition of a room of furniture and functional objects, all cut in half, was meant to suggest that memory and the realities in the mind are as potent and eternal as those of concrete, physical presences. Ono's ambition to alter the viewer's sense of reality is further apparent from her admonition to viewers to remain in the white room she had created for the exhibition "until it turns blue." That the reality Ono wished her audience to appreciate includes the immaterial is underscored by her warning caption on *Disappearing Piece* that "the object in this box will evaporate when the lid is opened."

The medium of film offered a particularly fruitful juncture for Ono's effort to poetically represent and interpret the ineffable nature of life. In her films Ono confronted the very foundation of cinema: its ability to record photographically what is in front of the lens. She sought to acknowledge the material process of film recording while simultaneously penetrating beyond the surface of the given image. For example, in her early Fluxus film, *No. 1 (Match)* (1966), the single gesture of lighting a match became a metaphor for the light of the projector and the illumination of its subject. Filling the screen, the match appeared within its own light and was consumed by the light-making process.

In challenging traditional notions of filmmaking, Ono was part of a general assault on film conventions which occurred during the 1960s—a formative period in the history of American independent film culture. The ways in which artists employed the cinematic apparatus (camera, film, projection system) radically shifted; instead of creating narratives or symbolic, hallucinatory dream states evoking the unconscious, filmmakers sought a direct acknowledgment of the material properties of film and the artifice of the production process.

Just as other artists moved between media in order to challenge the definition of performance and object-making, so too did filmmakers transform and redefine the traditional genres and characteristics of cinema. Some films defied the narrative structure and expectations of what constituted the cinematic experience and sought to dismantle traditional ideas of acting for the camera and the myth of the Hollywood "star." The Hollywood studio, for example, was parodied in the outrageous happeninglike films of Jack Smith (*Flaming Creatures*, 1963), while the star system was satirized by Andy Warhol's Factory, with its stable of underground movie stars. Artists also radically reconceptualized the idea of cinematic time: Warhol's *Eat* (1963), for example, is a forty-minute film which showed the artist Robert Indiana slowly eating one mushroom. The material of film itself was the source of Bruce Conner films, such as *A Movie* (1958), in which he reedited found footage to create witty deconstructions of the visual language of Hollywood and science films. These examples describe the vital precedents and context in which the Fluxus films produced and distributed by George Maciunas appeared. Yoko Ono's Fluxus films *Eyeblink, No. 1 (Match)*, and *No. 4 (Bottoms)* (all from 1966), like those of other Fluxus artists, provocatively debunked the authority of the camera and the tradition of passive spectatorship. As with her Fluxus colleagues, Ono sought to confront the viewer and to expose the fictions and realities of the camera's representation of the world around us.

Ono's first films emerged in the mid-1960s out of the same complex totality of interdisciplinary endeavors that had informed her objects and performances. The distinctive style of these films was due not only to their conceptual organization but to the fact that, like her earlier instructions pieces, each film originated as a visual idea which was articulated in a brief written statement. Indeed, many of Ono's early films took the form of film scripts in which the viewer was instructed in how to perceive or imagine a film. Thus, in *Film Script 5* (1964), Ono makes us create our own movie and forces us to realize how a film is composed and manipulated by instructing us to look at a particular action—"not to look at Rock Hudson, but only Doris Day." In *Film No. 1 (A Walk to Taj Mahal)* (1964), the camera and audience participate in various actions which blur the distinction between audience and film. The film consists of snowfall only. By identifying the camera with the audience, the audience feels as if they are the ones who are walking in the snow.

Ono produced sixteen films between 1966 and 1982. Her best-known and most-celebrated film, *No. 4* (1966), established her interest in the body and the filmic strategies she would pursue in representing it. Known as *Bottoms*, this film is composed of a series of shots of people's moving backsides, framed and edited so that the entire screen is filled with one bare bottom after another. The soundtrack that accompanied the second version is made up of the comments of the unidentified subjects of the film talking about the process of being filmed. In the following years Ono produced films, such as *Film No. 5 (Smile)* (1968), which celebrated her relationship with John Lennon, whom she had met in 1966. In *Two Virgins* (1968), Ono created short lyrical expressions of their love by filmically fusing images of their bodies.

Production photograph from *Film No. 5 (Smile)*, 1968.

Celebrity status and feminism became subtexts in another of Ono's most complex and engaging films, *Rape* (1969). This film took as its premise a conceptual idea that Ono gave to a camera crew: select a person at random and follow that person with a camera. The subject was a German-speaking woman in London whom the crew encountered and doggedly pursued to her apartment. The woman's initial curiosity and openness turned to frustration and anger as the camera relentlessly followed her. The uniqueness of this film derives from the viewers' confusion about what is happening on screen: is this woman, in fact, being pursued, or is she an actress? She does not speak English, yet we can understand her actions and emotions. This film explores issues of the camera as a transgressor of privacy, and, by extension, of the male film crew and ourselves as viewer-voyeur.

In 1970 and 1971, Ono created seven films that extended her conceptual, poetic, and narrative concerns. In *Up Your Legs Forever* (1970), repetition makes us aware of the particularities and differences of individual anatomies. In contrast to *Bottoms*, which featured a stationary camera and moving subjects, *Up Your Legs Forever* called for the camera to move up the legs of subjects who remained motionless. As with *Bottoms*, great variety is created without once varying the method of shooting the film. In *Fly* (1970), the subject is a fly, closely followed by the camera as it moves about the landscape of a nude body. Given that the projected film magnifies both fly and body, the close-up shots of the fly make us acutely aware of scale. Unlike *Bottoms* and *Up Your Legs Forever*, in which sound recordings of the production process make the anonymous subjects real and yet invisible, the soundtrack of *Fly* is a voice piece by Ono. Her distinctive song becomes the sound of the fly, and the expressive range of her voice invests the insect's movements with meaning. *Freedom* (1970), with its image of a woman pulling at the clasp of her bra, is a metaphor for the liberation of the female body and the self.

Two other films of this period, *Erection* (1971) and *Apotheosis* (1970), focus on the process of movement and change through time. *Erection* is a pixillated film—each sequence a series of still photographs shot from the same point of view over a period of time—showing a building gradually being erected on an empty lot in London. As time is collapsed and the action speeded up, the building seems to take on an organic form, "growing" before our eyes. In *Apotheosis*, we follow Ono and Lennon as they ascend in a balloon into the sky above a small town. In the gradual unfolding of the action in real time, the film becomes poetically evocative as the camera-balloon breaks through a cloud bank to the spectacularly clear vistas of the sky above. The sounds from the village are left behind as we enter the silent space above the earth.

In Ono's films, stripped as they are of the conventions of storytelling, the camera serves as an eye, an instrument for observation. Like her work in performance and sculpture, Ono's films acknowledge their materials—in this case, the image-producing properties of the film medium. This acknowledgment is apparent in Ono's emphasis on formal concerns: (1) the cropped, single-image composition in *No. 4 (Bottoms)*; (2) the articulation of movement through specific actions in *Fly*; (3) temporality, as expressed through repetition in *Up Your Legs Forever*, and through the animation of sequences of still photographs in *Erection*; (4) positing the camera as the protagonist in the creation of narrative in *Rape*; (5) the relationship between image and vocal sound in *Fly*. These formal devices are directed toward Ono's central concern with the image-recording process of the media and her exploration of strategies for representing the human body—both as a subject matter for the camera (*Fly, Bottoms, Up Your Legs Forever, Freedom*) and for the viewer's voyeurism (*Rape*).

Cinematic explorations formed a crucial outlet for Ono's aesthetic explorations between 1967 and 1971, when the Everson Museum in Syracuse, New York, offered her a retrospective. The exhibition provided the impetus to realize ideas that had previously existed only in concept and to fabricate work which no longer existed. But the circus atmosphere that surrounded the exhibition, caused by John Lennon's participation as guest artist, ultimately led Ono to abandon object-making on an ambitious scale for some eighteen years. As she later acknowledged, "That was the end of the quiet kind of conceptual games I was playing."

Henceforth, she channelled her energies into filmmaking and music, often in collaboration with Lennon. These activities retained the confrontational and poetic edge that had characterized her earlier work, but they now took place within the context of popular culture. Realizing the potential of this context, Ono joined with Lennon in a number of collaborative projects, such as *Bed-In* (1969) and *War Is Over* (1969), which used their celebrity status to draw attention to the peace movement. Imbued with a pervasive optimism in the power of imagination, these activities manifested Ono's longstanding belief that the "mind is omnipotent" and that all her work was a "form of wishing."

Perhaps the film which captured this spirit most completely was *Imagine* (1971), a feature-length evocation of Ono and Lennon's music and life-style. Here, their travels, their friends, and, most importantly, their music are the subjects. In *Imagine*, the camera is turned upon John and Yoko as they become part of the public imagination. The powers of cinematic observation transform the world of the self into spectacle, recording the public life of public people.

Ono's final cinematic productions were concert films—*Ten for Two: Sisters, O Sisters* (1972)—and music videos. Directed by Ono, these latter videos—*Walking on Thin Ice* (1981), *Woman* (1981), and *Goodbye Sadness* (1982)—were produced after John Lennon's death. A profound sense of loss fills these songs and images, which circulate between their past together and Ono's present life of separation. The recasting of that life through film and song creates a dialectic between history and memory, art and life.

In 1988, eighteen years after her Syracuse Show, Ono reestablished herself as an object-maker. Her reentry to the field was precipitated by an invitation to contribute to an exhibition in Cincinnati paying homage to John Cage on his seventy-fifth birthday. For the occasion, she made a bronze version of the 1966 work *Chess Set: For Playing as Long as You Can Remember Where All Your Pieces Are*. Enamelled to a uniform white, the new chess set, entitled *Play It By Trust*, bespeaks the fundamental similarity between people, and thus the foolishness of oppositional conflict.

Ono with her 1966 *Wrapped Chair*, in Milan, 1990.

Two years later, inspired by an offer of an exhibition from the Whitney Museum of American Art, Ono replicated more than a dozen of her earlier works in bronze. Transparencies were rendered opaque; metamorphosis was arrested; and chance and audience participation were nullified—an act which dramatically changed the nature and meaning of the works. Seen together, the original version and the bronzes spoke to the paradox of objects that are at once the same and different. This theme was not new to Ono, but it had been given renewed focus by a visit to a restored palace outside Leningrad. Each room of the palace had two photographs on the wall—one taken in the czarist period and the other taken after the palace had been bombed by the Nazis. The three states of the room—two in the past and one in the present—were totally different; only the idea of the room remained the same.

While the buoyant aspect of Ono's early pieces spoke to a quality of the 1960s, bronze epitomized the 1980s, which Ono feels was an age of solidity and commodification. Transformation remained the underlying subject of these works, but she had transferred her arena from natural phenomena to social consciousness. The series, in her words, was "a story of change and survival. It was a story of all of us."

INSTRUCTION PIECES

> Instruction painting separates painting into two different functions: the instructions and the realization. The work becomes a reality only when others realize the work. Instructions can be realized by different people in many different ways. This allows infinite transformation of the work that the artist himself cannot foresee, and brings the concept of "time" into painting. It immediately eliminates the usual emphasis put on the original painting, and art comes down from the pedestal. . . .
>
> Instruction painting makes it possible to explore the invisible, the world beyond the existing concept of time and space. And then, sometimes later, the instructions themselves will disappear and be properly forgotten.
>
> y.o. from *Yoko at Indica*, Indica Gallery, London, 1966

Ono's first two- and three-dimensional works, which she called instruction paintings, relied on chance and audience participation; consequently, they incorporated metamorphosis and mutability.

By providing situations which gave viewers license to express their creative potential, Ono sought to underscore the nonexclusive nature of creativity. For her, "everyone on earth has creativity," and thus everyone has the potential to be an artist. "Being an artist," she stated, "involves only having a certain frame of mind, an attitude, determination, and imagination that springs naturally out of the necessity of the situation."

Ono included a number of her instruction paintings in her first exhibition in New York in July 1961 at the AG Gallery. Because so few people attended the exhibition, Ono was able to verbally describe to every viewer the instructional component of each piece. At subsequent presentations, she relied exclusively on written instructions placed next to her objects.

Painting to Be Stepped On

Leave a piece of canvas or finished painting on the floor or in the street.

y.o. 1960 winter

A Work to Be Stepped On, 1961

Photo © George Maciunas

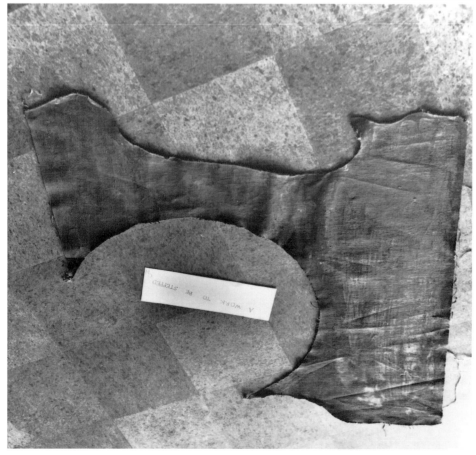

This painting stems from FUMIE, meaning "stepping painting."
In the 15th century in Japan during the persecution of the Christians by the feudal lords, suspected Christians were lined up and asked to step on a painting of Christ or the Virgin Mary. Those who would not step on the painting were crucified.

y.o. from *Yoko at Indica*, Indica Gallery, London, 1966

A Plus B Painting

Cut out a circle on canvas A.
Place a numerical figure, a roman letter, or a katakana on canvas B on an arbitrary point.
Place canvas A on canvas B and hang them together.
The figure on canvas B may show, may show partially, or may not show.
You may use old paintings, photographs, etc. instead of blank canvases.

y.o. 1961 autumn

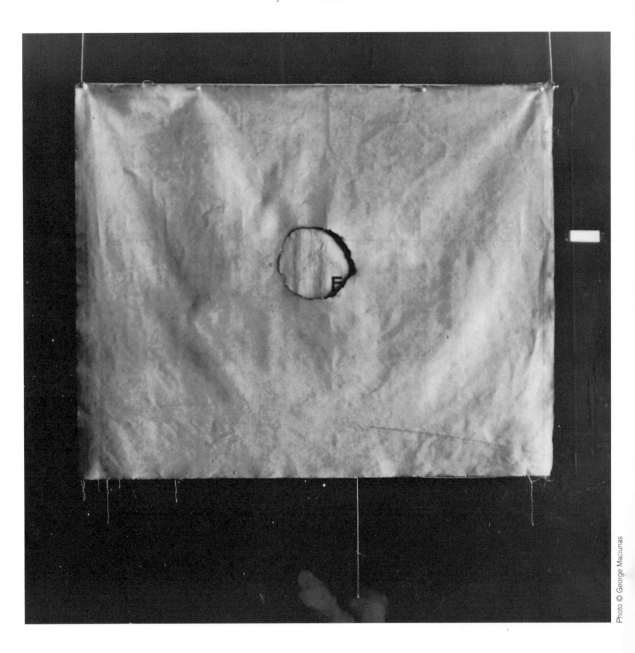

A + B Painting, 1961

Ono was intrigued with the visual power of words to evoke meaning through fragments—as in a city where words are partially blocked by objects in front of them. Fueled by a desire to translate the mystery of this urban landscape into visual art, she cut a circular aperture in one canvas which opened to a second canvas on which a letter had been inscribed. In this way, Ono evoked the existence of a word whose remaining letters are hidden from view.

Painting to Shake Hands
(Painting for Cowards)

Drill a hole in a canvas and put your hand out from behind.
Receive your guests in that position.
Shake hands and converse with hands.

y.o. 1961 autumn

Painting to Shake Hands, 1966 (realization of 1961 script)

Subtitled *Painting for a Coward*, Ono intended this piece for people who were too shy to shake hands without hiding, or who wanted to share only one part of themselves. Ono considered this "way of saying hello" to be a metaphor for art. Underneath the lofty aspirations of the artist, she felt, lay the desire to eradicate loneliness by communicating with others. "What are artists actually doing? We just want some kind of communication through our loneliness. This is really what painting is: it is like shaking hands—with individuals we see only through our work."

In *Add Colour Painting* and *Kitchen Piece*, Ono conflated viewer and performer by turning over to viewers the responsibility for creating the paintings by adding the proffered materials—colour and food respectively—to the canvases. Such an overt call for viewer participation challenged traditional assumptions about the art object as well as about the sanctity of artistic authorship.

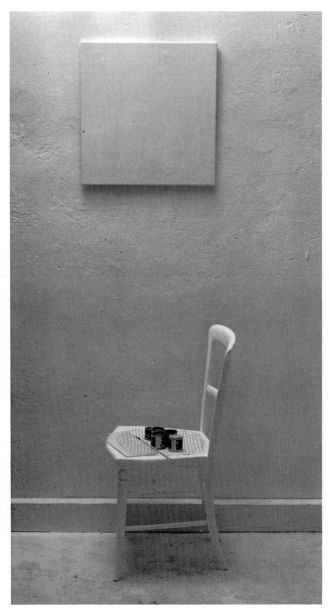

Add Colour Painting, 1966

Kitchen Piece, 1966 (realization of 1960 script)

Kitchen Piece

Hang a canvas on a wall.
Throw all the leftovers you have in the
    kitchen that day on the canvas.
You may prepare special food for the piece.

y.o. 1960 winter

Painting to Hammer a Nail

Hammer a nail into a mirror, a piece of glass, a canvas, wood or metal every morning. Also, pick up a hair that came off when you combed in the morning and tie it around the hammered nail. The painting ends when the surface is covered with nails.

y.o. 1961 winter

Painting to Hammer a Nail

Hammer a nail in the center of a piece of glass.
Send each fragment to an arbitrary address.

y.o. 1962 spring

Painting to Hammer a Nail, 1966 (realization of 1961 script)

When 'Hammer A Nail' painting was exhibited at Indica Gallery, a person came and asked if it was alright to hammer a nail in the painting. I said it was alright if he pays 5 shillings. Instead of paying the 5 shillings, he asked if it was alright for him to hammer an imaginary nail in. That was John Lennon. I thought, so I met a guy who plays the same game I played.

y.o. from *Yoko Ono at Lisson,* Lisson Gallery, London, 1967

Film Script 3
(unrealized)

Ask audience to cut the part of the image on the screen that they don't like.

Supply scissors.

y.o. 1964

Film Script 4
(unrealized)

Ask audience to stare at the screen until it becomes black.   y.o. 1964

Film Script 5
(unrealized)

Ask audience the following:
1) not to look at Rock Hudson, but only Doris Day.

2) not to look at any round objects but only square and angled objects—if you look at a round object watch it until it becomes square and angled.

3) not to look at blue, but only red—If blue comes out, close eyes or do something so you do not see. If you saw it, then make believe that you have not seen it.

y.o. 1964

My paintings, which are all instruction paintings (and meant for others to do), came after collage & assemblage (1915) and happening (1905) came into the art world. Considering the nature of my painting, any of the above three words or a new word can be used instead of the word, painting. But I like the old word painting because it immediately connects with "wall painting" painting, and it is nice and funny.

Among my instruction paintings, my interest is mainly in "painting to construct in your head." In your head, for instance, it is possible for a straight line to exist—not as a segment of a curve but as a straight line. Also, a line can be straight, curved and something else at the same time. A dot can exist as a 1, 2, 3, 4, 5, 6, dimensional object all at the same time or at various times in different combinations as you wish to perceive. The movement of the molecule can be continuum and discontinuum at the same time. It can be with color and/or without. There is no visual object that does not exist in comparison to or simultaneously with other objects, but these characteristics can be eliminated if you wish. A sunset can go on for days. You can eat up all the clouds in the sky. You can assemble a painting with a person in the North Pole over a phone, like playing chess. The painting method derives from as far back as the time of the Second World War when we had no food to eat, and my brother and I exchanged menus in the air.

•   •   •

There may be a dream that two dream together, but there is no chair that two see together.

Excerpts from Ono's *To the Wesleyan People*, 1966

Painting to Hammer a Nail, 1990

In 1990, Ono restaged *Painting to Hammer a Nail* at the Judson Memorial Church, New York. Ono had long claimed that her work was "a form of wishing." Her introduction of the crucifix image specifically connected this piece to the ritualistic quality of prayer she had witnessed as a child: "As a child in Japan, I used to go to a temple and write out a wish on a piece of thin paper and tie it in a knot around the branch of a tree. Trees in temple courtyards were always filled with people's wish knots, which looked like white flowers blossoming from afar."

NATURE: FLUX AND

Ono's early work is characterized by its direct incorporation of natural process. Nature, in Ono's lexicon, is a paradigm for the flux which informs all of life. For Ono, everything is in constant motion; what we perceive as static is, in reality, moving — even if only on a molecular level. Ono's desire to aesthetically capture this flux led her to treat transformation and the passage of time as subjects of her art.

Painting to Let the Evening Light Go Through, 1966 (realization of 1961 script)

TRANSFORMATION

Painting to Let the Evening Light Go Through

Hang a bottle behind a canvas.
Place the canvas where the west light comes in.
The painting will exist when the bottle creates a shadow on the canvas, or it does not have to exist.
The bottle may contain liquor, water, grasshoppers, ants or singing insects, or it does not have to contain.

y.o. 1961 summer

Have You Seen a Horizon Lately

Have you seen a horizon lately
If you have, watch it for awhile
For you never know
It may not last so long

Have you seen an evening light lately
If you have, watch it for awhile
For you never know
It may not be the same

Have you seen a snowflake lately
If you have, hold it in your hand
For you never know
It may melt away

Have you been in love lately
If you have, hold it in your heart
For you never know
It may be the last

y.o. 1973; song included in *Approximately Infinite Universe*

Ono's embrace of evanescent natural phenomena is particularly evident in her pieces involving light, which she considered too complex to be rendered successfully by human means. "Only the evening light can create the evening light," she remarked. "The shimmer of the evening light is so beautiful that it is something beyond our creation. Once you represent it—and render it static—you destroy its quality." By calling upon nature itself to serve as both the subject and object of her work, Ono avoided the disparity between "the beautiful, mysterious thing that we appreciate in nature and the far less complex thing that we create in art." By so doing, she "gave the canvas to the evening light rather than trying to create the evening light on canvas."

The idea of conflating agent and subject in an artwork originated with Ono's desire to include the sound of birds in one of her musical compositions and her realization that the bird song was too complex to notate in a musical score. "From an early age, I had a habit that whenever I heard a sound, I would see it in a music score—as notation. But you could not possibly translate the bird song into musical notations because it was too complex." She abandoned the attempt to replicate the bird's sound through notation and, instead, sought a means by which the bird could create its own sound. The result was a musical piece directing performers to play a note while letting a bird sing.

Wind Piece

Make a way for the wind.

This was first performed in 1962 at the Sogetsu Art Center, Tokyo, with a huge electric fan on the stage. In 1966 at Wesleyan University, Connecticut, the audience was asked to move their chairs a little and make a narrow aisle for the wind to pass through. No wind was created with special means.

y.o.

Mailing Piece III

Send a wind around the world many times until it becomes a very delicate breeze.

y.o. 1962 summer

Painting for the Wind

Cut a hole in a bag filled with seeds of any kind and place the bag where there is wind.

y.o. 1961 summer

Photo © George Maciunas

Painting for the Wind, 1961

Painting for the Wind provides a framework for the wind, blowing through the hole in the canvas, to scatter the seeds that are contained in the suspended bag. The physical components of the piece are thus simply props or instruments for the real "action" of the work: the dispersing of the seeds into the world and their eventual growth into trees. Conceptually, the work concerns itself with time and transformation. By literally incorporating natural elements into her art, Ono avoids the problem of static depictions of organic processes.

Always alert to the musical potential in purportedly nonmusical situations, Ono allowed for the inclusion of sound and movement in two versions of the piece which called for a "fine bamboo screen" to be placed in front of the hole. Such a screen would presumably flutter and create noise when placed in a strong wind.

Painting in Three Stanzas

Let a vine grow.
Water every day.

The first stanza — till the vine spreads.
The second stanza — till the vine withers.
The third stanza — till the wall vanishes.

y.o. 1961 summer

Photo © George Maciunas

Painting in Three Stanzas, 1961

Ono's technique of stimulating the viewer's sensate capacities by reversing the normal means by which we process sensory information is concretely articulated in *Painting in Three Stanzas*. Here, she conceptually identifies the sound of a vine growing with a three-part musical composition.

Pea Piece

Carry a bag of peas. Leave a pea wherever
you go.

y.o. 1960 winter

Mailing Piece II

Send the sound of one hundred sun[s]
    rising at once.

                                       y.o.

Ono with *Wish Piece*, 1973–90

Make a wish when the sun hits   y.o.

Tunafish Sandwich Piece

Imagine one thousand suns in the
    sky at the same time.
Let them shine for one hour.
Then, let them gradually melt
    into the sky.
Make one tunafish sandwich and eat.

                                    y.o. 1964 spring

Snow Piece

Think that snow is falling.
Think that snow is falling
    everywhere all the time.
When you talk with a person,
    think that snow is falling
    between you and on the person.
Stop conversing when you
    think the person is covered by snow.

y.o. 1963 summer

Tape Piece III
Snow Piece

Take a tape of the sound of the snow
    falling.
This should be done in the evening.
Do not listen to the tape.
Cut it and use it as strings to tie gifts with.
Make a gift wrapper, if you wish, using the
    same process with a phonosheet.

y.o. 1963 autumn

Film No. 1
A Walk to Taj Mahal (second version)
(never realized)

The film consists of snowfall only. The camera will make a walk movement of a person in the snow. The camera will move sometimes in a circle, sometimes zigzag, sometimes slow, but mostly, will be at a normal speed. Then at the last point, it will go up to the sky. It should make the audience feel as if they are the ones who are walking in the snow and who go up into the sky.

This should take something like an hour for the total walk.

For the sound, ask the audience to hold bunches of white flowers and pick them slowly.

y.o. 1964

Water Piece

Steal a moon on the water with a bucket.
Keep stealing until no moon is seen on the
    water.

y.o. 1964 spring

I Love You, Earth

I love you, Earth
You are beautiful
I love the way you are
I know I never said it to you
But I wanna say it now
I love you, I love you, I love you, Earth
I love you, I love you, I love you, now

I love you, Earth
You are beautiful
I love the way you shine
I love your vallies, I love your mornings
In fact I love you every day
I know I never said it to you
Why, I would never know
Over blue mountains, over greenfields
I wanna scream about it now

I love you, I love you, I love you, Earth
I love you, I love you, I love you, now
You are our meeting point of infinity
You are our turning point in eternity
I love you, I love you, I love you, Earth
I love you, I love you, I love you, now

y.o. 1985; song included in *Starpeace*

Sun Piece

Watch the sun until
    it becomes square.

y.o. 1962 winter

Smoke Painting

Light canvas or any finished painting with a
    cigarette at any time for any length of
    time.
See the smoke movement.
The painting ends when the whole canvas
    or painting is gone.

y.o. 1961 summer

EARLY PERFORMANCE

Ono performing
Voice Piece for Soprano, c. 1961.

Voice Piece for Soprano
to Simone Morris

Scream.

1. against the wind
2. against the wall
3. against the sky

y.o. 1961 autumn

Initially, Ono's performance works took the form of written scripts. In this state, they resembled short and often paradoxical poetry. They sought to engender a mental state of complete relaxation by eliminating complexity and concentrating, instead, on single aspects of experience or perception—or, as Ono described it, "sensory experience isolated from other sensory experiences."

Ono's first public music performance took place at the Village Gate, New York in 1961. In addition to *A Grapefruit in the World of Park*, she included several compositions whose sounds were those that unintentionally occurred in the process of executing matter-of-fact tasks. As by-products of another activity—"by-sound" or "insound," as Ono dubbed them—these noises avoided self-conscious, subjective expression in favor of "real" sound.

WORK

Ono's Village Gate concert was followed by a solo evening of performances, presented at the Carnegie Recital Hall on November 24, 1961, and restaged at the Sogetsu Art Center in Tokyo in 1962. These concerts comprised three pieces: *A Grapefruit in the World of Park, A Piece for Strawberries and Violins* (see descriptions pp. 4, 5 respectively) and *AOS*. In this later work, Ono wrapped two performers in gauze, back to back, and dangled an assortment of empty bottles and cans from their ankles and waists. Their instructions were to walk from one end of the stage to the other, without making any noise. This injunction against sound, coupled with the difficulty of one performer moving backwards while the other moved forward, caused them to move extremely slowly—an effect which resembled a slow-motion film.

Wall Piece I

Sleep two walls away from each other.
Whisper to each other.

y.o. 1963 autumn

Ono's 1965 concert at Carnegie Recital Hall in New York was a series of Events, the most arresting of which was *Cut Piece* (see description pp. 90-92). Among the other Events performed were *Bag Piece,* in which Ono and a male assistant crawled into a huge black bag, removed their clothes, and took a nap while another performer rode a bicycle slowly around the auditorium and across the stage. Ono and her assistant redressed in the bag and exited, taking the bag with them. Other inclusions were *Strip-tease for Three,* in which three wooden chairs were spotlighted on an empty stage, and *Snake Piece from AOS,* which began with the announcement that a snake had been let loose in the darkened auditorium; from time to time, strange noises were heard as one performer, bound and dragging chains, hobbled across the stage. The program ended with *Clock Piece,* in which a clock was placed at center stage and the audience was told that the piece would end when the alarm rang. Those members of the audience who went up to the stage to investigate discovered the clock had neither arms nor alarm.

Lyric accompaniment to *A Grapefruit in the World of Park*

WHERE IS THIS
THIS IS THE PARK
I CAN SMELL METAL IN THE AIR
NO ITS THE CLOVERS
ARE THEY BLEEDING
NO ITS THE SUNSET
IS THIS THE ROOM
NO ITS THE SUNSET
WOULD YOU LIKE TO SPEAK TO THE DEAD
OH NO
I ONLY CAME HERE TO PEEL GRAPEFRUIT
IS IT TOO COLD
ITS TOO WARM
THE SKYS TOO HIGH
PEOPLE TURNING UP THEIR STOMACHS
CONTENTEDLY TO THE SKY
YOUR VOICE SOUNDS UNUSUALLY SMALL IN
THE AFTERNOON AIR
YOUR MINDS FLY AWAY BETWEEN THE
CLOUDS AND THE DROPPING DEW ON YOUR
CHEEKS IS LIKE THE KISSES OF YOUR
LOVERS
DRINK PEPSI COLA YOU'LL LIKE IT IT LIKES
YOU
DON'T PEEL IT
EVERYTHING SEEMS SO RIGHT IN THE PARK—
YES DOESN'T IT
EVEN THE GRAPEFRUIT OH NO NOT THE
GRAPEFRUIT YES EVEN THE GRAPEFRUIT.
WHY DON'T YOU THROW IT AWAY ITS
WRINKLED
ITS WRINKLED

2
LETS COUNT THE HAIRS OF THE DEAD CHILD
LETS COUNT THE HAIRS OF THE DEAD CHILD
DO YOU LIKE CLAMS
I LIKE CLAMS ONLY ITS HARD TO PEEL THEM
THOUGH
PEEL CLAMS
OH YES YOU DO
ITS GOOD FOR YOU THEY SAY
I DIDN'T KNOW THAT
I MUST TRY THAT SOMETIMES
NOW DON'T HURT YOUR FINGERS
NO I WON'T
THEY LOOK SO JUICY
NOW LETS TRY
HOW IS IT
WELL I PREFER METROCAL TO CLAMS AT
LEAST ITS SOMETHING DIFFERENT
DINNERS READY
DID YOU HEAR THAT
HAVE TO ASK ME
SOMETIMES ITS TOO MUCH ISN'T IT
YES ITS JUST TOO MUCH FOR ME
LETS COUNT THE HAIRS OF THE DEAD CHILD
LETS COUNT THE HAIRS OF THE DEAD CHILD
9

3

I HAVE TO SQUEEZE LEMONS
YES
WE MUST LIVE
WE MUST DO SOMETHING
SOMETHING CONSTRUCTIVE I GUESS
LETS NOT LEAVE THE ROOM LETS STAY LETS
LIVE LONGER
SO WE CAN DRINK TEA TOGETHER
THAT'D BE NICE
BUT THATS A DREAM
6   2   21
JO JO IS THAT YOUR TIE FLY IN THE SKY
OH NO ITS THE LOCK ISN'T IT
BUT LOCKS DON'T FLY UP INTO THE SKY
WHO'S JO
OH I'VE NEVER MET HIM BUT I KNOW THAT HE
HAS LONG FINGERS
LONG NAILS TOO NO JUST LONG FINGERS
AND HE CAN SQUEEZE LEMONS VERY WELL
I HEARD HIS VOICE ONCE LIKE FRAGMENTS
OF BROKEN MIRROR
ITS SAD THAT WE CAN'T KEEP VOICES LIKE
WE KEEP MUSHROOMS
ONE
ITS GETTING DARK
THE FLOWERS ARE STILL WHITE THOUGH
ARE THEY WASTE PAPERS

4

IS THIS THE PARK
CAN YOU OPEN THE WINDOW
CAN YOU OPEN THE WINDOW
ITS LOCKED
ITS LOCKED
LOOK THE CLOUD IS MOVING
IT WAS BETWEEN THOSE TREES BEFORE SEE
ARE YOU BLEEDING
ONE DAY HIS BONES TOUCHED MINE
I WAS HAPPY
YOU LIKE BONES YES THEY MAKE YOU FEEL
COMFORTABLE I GUESS
WIPE YOUR FINGERS ON THE GRASS ITS
STICKY
THE LOLLIPOPS ARE GETTING SOFT
DO YOU LIKE MY BABY CARRIAGE
OH ITS SIMPLY WONDERFUL
THE CURVE THE SHINY WHEELS
EVERYTHINGS JUST RIGHT
IS IT EMPTY

Poster for Ono's concert at the Carnegie Recital Hall, New York, November 24, 1961.

I SHINE IT EVERY DAY WITH VINEGAR AND TAKE OFF THE SMELL WITH PERFUMES
DID YOU KNOW I HAD TO GET THIS FOOD FOR $10 HOW CAN YOU GIVE $10 FOR THIS MANY. I WANTED TO MAKE IT NICER YOU KNOW NOT GRAPEFRUITS OR CLAMS ANYWAY. WHAT CAN YOU DO. WELL IT MAKES YOU FEEL GOOD TO DO SOMETHING FOR OTHERS YOU KNOW. I AM NOT COMPLAINING OF BEING IN CHARGE OF THESE THINGS.

5

ARE YOU LISTENING
YOU LOOK SO PALE I GUESS ITS THIS LIGHT
ARE YOU DEAD
18
18
ITS CLOSING
ITS CLOSING
ARE YOU BLEEDING
LETS GO
LETS NOT GO
IS IT TOO WRINKLED
STOP PEELING
PEASE PORRIDGE HOT
PEASE PORRIDGE COLD
PEASE PORRIDGE IN THE PARK
NINE DAYS OLD
BETSY STOP THAT WERE GOING NOW
SOME LIKE IT HOT
SOME LIKE IT COLD
OH YES YES I MUST REMEMBER THAT
IT IS SO HARD TO KEEP TRACK OF THINGS
YOU KNOW
THEY ALL GO
ARE WE GOING MUMMY
YOUR COLLAR IS PERSPIRING YOU'LL CATCH COLD PUSSY

6

WHY DON'T YOU PUT ON YOUR SWEATER
I'M HOT MUMMY CAN I HAVE SOMETHING TO DRINK
THEY'RE ALL GONE HONEY
NOW PUT ON YOUR JACKET TOO ITS GETTING CHILLY
CLOSING
3
I'M TIRED
IS THE PARK GONE
DID IT GET TIRED OF US
THE GRAPEFRUIT IS STILL SHINING ON THE TABLE
THE SEEDS THE PIECES OF HARD SKIN
IS THAT YOUR HAIR LYING ON THE FLOOR OR IS THAT THE GRASS
ITS WET ISN'T IT
DOES IT EVER DRY
THE ROOM IS FILLED WITH LIGHT
NO OTHER ROOM IS FULL OF HAIRS
THE WIND HAS STOLEN MY KEY
CAN WE EVER GET OUT
WHERE'S MY LEMONADE
ARE YOU DEAD
OH NO THANK YOU
I ONLY CAME HERE TO PEEL YOU
JO
JO

of Park

y.o.

*_____ Piece from AOS

Theatre or auditorium is without light.

It is announced that members of audience must find their own means of light for the "…search…"

It is announced that a snake, butterfly, rabbit, grapefruit or a body, or anything the announcer thought he wished to see on the day of the production, has been released or hidden in the audience and the audience must find it.

Two performers who have been tightly bound together with rope then proceed from one wing or side of the stage to the other wing or side and back as quickly as possible and without making any audible sound.

The two performers must be tightly bound together, back to back, or front to front, or side to side, or with one performer upside down, or in any position in which they may be tightly bound together. Attached to their bounds must be tin cans, bottles or any objects that would make noise upon movement.

*The title of the piece is to be that word which the announcer has chosen to say has been released or hidden. Whatever it is, it should not actually be released or hidden, but only announced to that effect.

y.o.

Bicycle Piece for Orchestra

Ride bicycles anywhere you can in the concert hall.
Do not make any noise.

y.o. 1962 autumn

Laundry Piece

In entertaining your guests, bring out your laundry of the day and explain to them about each item.
How and when it became dirty and why, etc.

y.o. 1963 summer

Touch Poem for Group of People

Touch each other.

y.o. 1963 winter

The several versions of Ono's performance Touch Poems shared their title with another series of Touch Poems which Ono created by writing words on a piece of paper and then blocking out parts of the words with paper overlays. She eventually found that these raised-paper overlays had an independent, three-dimensional quality, and she began to focus exclusively on the raised paper. Her success at creating a poetry that was accessible only by touch encouraged her to paste other elements—such as locks of her hair—onto the page as if to create tactile illustrations of the invisible poems.

Mirror Piece

Instead of obtaining a mirror,
    obtain a person.
Look into him.
Use different people.
Old, young, fat, small, etc.

        y.o. 1964 spring

Lighting Piece

Light a match and watch
    till it goes out.

        y.o. 1965 autumn

Ono performing *Lighting Piece* at the Sogetsu School of Ikebana, Tokyo, 1962.

Stone Piece

Find a stone that is your size or weight.
Crack it until it becomes fine powder.
Dispose of it in the river. (a)
Send small amounts to your friends. (b)
Do not tell anybody what you did.
Do not explain about the powder to the
    friends to whom you send.

        y.o. 1963 winter

Question Piece

Question.

This piece was first performed in Tokyo, 1962, at the Sogetsu Art Center, by two people on stage asking questions to each other and not answering. At the time it was done in French, but it can be done in any language or in many different languages at one time. The piece is meant for a dialogue or a monologue of continuous questions, answered only by questions. It was also performed in English on Voice of America Radio Program, Tokyo, 1964, and in Japanese on NTV (Japanese Television) by six children from the audience, 1964.

y.o.

On occasion, Ono performed in the works of other artists. Here, she brought individual interpretations to one of John Cage's compositions performed at the Sogetsu School of Ikebana, Tokyo, October 9, 1962.

Beat Piece

Listen to a heart beat.

y.o. 1963 autumn

Walk Piece

Stir inside of your brains
 with a penis until
 things are mixed well.
Take a walk.

y.o. 1961 winter

Laugh Piece

Keep laughing a week.

y.o. 1961 winter

Wall Piece for Orchestra

Hit a wall with your head.

y.o. 1962 winter

Collecting Piece

Collect sounds in your mind that you have
 overheard through the week.
Repeat them in your mind in different orders
 one afternoon.

y.o. 1963 autumn

A Piece for Orchestra

Count all the stars of that night by heart.
The piece ends when all the orchestra members finish counting the stars, or when it dawns.
This can be done with windows instead of stars.

y.o. 1962 summer

John Cage, David Tudor, Ono and Toshiro Mayuzumi in Cage's *Music Walk*, performed at the Sogetsu School of Ikebana, Tokyo, October 9, 1962.

Concert Piece

When the curtain rises, go hide and wait until everybody leaves you.
Come out and play.

y.o. 1963 autumn

Strip Tease for Three

First version for curtain:
Curtain rises to show three chairs placed on stage.
Curtain descends.

Second version for no curtain:
Single performer places three chairs on stage one at a time.
Performer removes chairs one at a time.

y.o.

At another time, also in Kyoto, before the Nanzenji Event, I had a concert at Yamaichi Hall. It was called "The Strip-tease Show" (it was stripping of the mind). When I met the High Monk the next day, he seemed a bit dissatisfied.

"I went to your concert" he said.
"Thank you, did you like it?"
"Well, why did you have those three chairs on the stage and call it a strip-tease by three?"
"If it is a chair or stone or woman, it is the same thing, my Monk."
"Where is the music?"
"The music is in the mind, my Monk."
"But that is the same with what we are doing, aren't you an avant-garde composer?"
"That is a label which was put by others for convenience."
"For instance, does Toshiro Mayuzumi create music of your kind?"
"I can only speak for myself."
"Do you have many followers?"
"No, but I know of two men who know what I am doing. I am very thankful for that."

Though he is a High Monk, he is extremely young, he may be younger than I. I wonder what the Monk is doing now.

Excerpt from Ono's *To the Wesleyan People*, 1966

Strip-tease for Three,
Carnegie Recital Hall, New York, 1965.

Clock Piece

Listen to the clock strokes.
Make exact repetitions in your head
    after they stop.

y.o. 1963 autumn

Clock Piece

Make all the clocks in the
    world fast by two
    seconds without letting
    anyone know about it.

y.o. 1963 winter

Clock Piece

Select a clock.
Set it on time.
You may rewind the clock
    but never reset it.
Call it your life clock.
Live accordingly.

y.o. 1964 spring

Clock Piece

Alarm clock is placed on the stage and set to ring at an undisclosed time.
It is announced that the piece will be finished when the alarm clock rings.

y.o.

An audience member examining the clock in *Clock Piece*, Carnegie Recital Hall, New York, March 21, 1965.

Ono in *Morning Piece, 1964* (to George Maciunas); performed in 1965.

Ono's performance work *Morning Piece, 1964* (to George Maciunas) pays homage to the sunrise. Participants in the piece were asked to come to the roof of Ono's residence at 87 Christopher Street before sunrise. Tacked to the door leading to the roof was a label imprinted with the words "enter sky," as if to establish that the actions conducted on the other side of the door existed outside the world of everyday reality. Once on the roof, participants were greeted by a table holding fragments of glass, each inscribed with a date—in the past or the future—which participants could purchase.

Ono's admonition to "wash your ears before you come" reversed the expectations about how one normally experiences the sunrise. By setting up a situation in which one would listen to rather than see a sunrise, Ono hoped to precipitate a new appreciation of the natural occurrence.

All my works in the other fields have an "Event bent," so to speak. People ask me why I call some works Event and others not. They also ask me why I do not call my Events, Happenings.

Event, to me, is not an assimilation of all other arts as Happening seems to be, but an extrication from the various sensory perceptions. It is not "a get togetherness" as most Happenings are, but a dealing with oneself. Also, it has no script as Happenings do, though it has something that starts it moving—the closest word for it may be a "wish" or "hope."

• • •

After unblocking one's mind, by dispensing with visual, auditory, and kinetic perceptions, what will come out of us? Would there be anything? I wonder. And my Events are mostly spent in wonderment.

• • •

People talk about happening. They say that art is headed towards that direction, that happening is assimilating the arts. I don't believe in collectivism of art nor in having only one direction in anything. I think it is nice to return to having many different arts, including happening, just as having many flowers. In fact, we could have more arts: "smell," "weight," "taste," "cry," "anger," (competition of anger, that sort of thing), etc. People might say that we never experience things separately, they are always in fusion, and that is why "the happening," which is a fusion of all sensory perceptions. Yes, I agree, but if that is so, it is all the more reason and challenge to create a sensory experience isolated from other sensory experiences, which is something rare in daily life. Art is not merely a duplication of life. To assimilate art in life is different from art duplicating life.

But returning to having various divisions of art does not mean, for instance, that one must use only sounds as means to create music. One may give instructions to watch the fire for ten days in order to create a vision in one's mind.

The mind is omnipresent, events in life never happen alone and the history is forever increasing its volume. The natural state of life and mind is complexity. At this point, what art can offer (if it can at all—to me it seems) is an absence of complexity, a vacuum through which you are led to a state of complete relaxation of mind. After that you may return to the complexity of life again, it may not be the same, or it may be, or you may never return, but that is your problem.

Mental richness should be worried just as physical richness. Didn't Christ say that it was like a camel trying to pass through a needle hole, for John Cage to go to heaven? I think it is nice to abandon what you have as much as possible, as many mental possessions as the physical ones, as they clutter your mind. It is nice to maintain poverty of environment, sound, thinking and belief. It is nice to keep oneself small, like a grain of rice, instead of expanding. Make yourself dispensable, like paper. See little, hear little, and think little.

The body is the Bodhi Tree The mind like a bright mirror standing Take care to wipe it all the time And allow no dust to cling. —*Shen-hsiu*	There never was a Bodhi Tree Nor bright mirror standing Fundamentally, not one thing exists So where is the dust to cling? —*Hui-neng*

Excerpts from Ono's *To the Wesleyan People*, 1966

LONDON

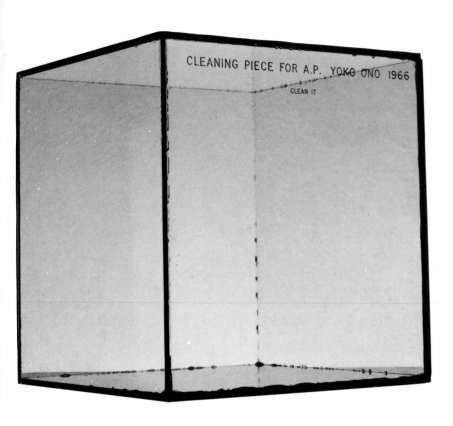

Cleaning Piece for A.P., 1966

In 1966, Ono opened a one-person exhibition at the Indica Gallery in London. Among the objects included in the show were fabrications in plexiglass of earlier instruction pieces as well as new performance-objects.

In October 1967, at the Lisson Gallery, Ono opened her second London exhibition. Entitled "Half-a-Wind Show," it was dominated by an everyday, household interior whose furniture and contents had been cut in half and painted a uniform white. For Ono, the environment operated on two levels. In the physical realm, it manifested her view that our vision reveals only partial views of reality: "everything we see is just the tip of the iceberg." Metaphysically, it alluded to her feelings of emptiness about her life. "I was feeling like a half at the time. The other side of me was empty. The piece was a reflection of the metaphysical room within me." In Ono's view, this metaphysical emptiness was answered by the entrance into her life of John Lennon, whom she describes as "the other half of me." Without the existence of this piece, Ono believes her autobiography would have been different.

After John Lennon saw the works to be included in Ono's "Half-a-Wind Show," he suggested that she sell the invisible half of her half-a-matter objects in bottles. As Ono acknowledged, "It was such a beautiful idea I decided to use it even though it was not mine."

EXHIBITIONS: 1966 1967

Ono with *Ceiling Painting* (also known as *Yes*), 1966.

Ceiling Painting (Yes) was included in Ono's Indica Gallery exhibition. Installed on the ceiling, it was inscribed with the word "yes," which was perceptible only by climbing up the ladder and reading the letters with a magnifying glass.

Apple, 1966

Time and metamorphosis, the underlying subjects of all of Ono's instruction pieces, were central to *Apple,* which Ono included in her Indica Gallery presentation. Ono's goal in presenting a real apple on a pedestal was to embody the cycle of nature. She envisioned the apple shrinking and eventually disintegrating. Only its seeds would remain on the pedestal, and these would be blown through the air and would later sprout into apple trees. John Lennon's response to the piece when he saw it was to take a bite out of the apple. "I didn't expect that," Ono later said. "It was an interruption of the piece that I had not planned. I was very upset at the time. But now I think it was a very interesting thing that happened: the cycle of organic change was interrupted by human action." Ono's 1989 bronze version of *Apple* immortalized the bite which Lennon had taken out of the original apple.

Fittingly, natural process and organic evolution were the subjects of the first artistic collaboration between Ono and John Lennon: two acorns which they entered as sculpture in an invitational exhibition in London. Unable to persuade the exhibition sponsors to include the acorns in the main exhibition space, Ono and Lennon requested that the seeds be planted in an adjacent grass area. For Ono, the planting of the seeds represented both the union of two artists as well as the union of polar opposites: East/West and man/woman. As she stated it, the piece "brought together the dichotomous forces of life."

Hide-Mouth

Hide your mouth at all times. The government should pass a law to prohibit such indecent exposure.   y.o. 1965

Cover of *Yoko at Indica*, Indica Gallery, London, 1966

The catalogue cover for Ono's Indica Gallery exhibition, "Unfinished Paintings and Objects by Yoko Ono," documented *Hide-Mouth,* one of the events she performed during the run of the exhibition. It consisted of Ono covering her mouth and that of her fellow performers in order to ridicule the idea that certain parts of the body were obscene while others were not. To Ono, the human body was beautiful in all its aspects. It is usually what is said rather than what is seen which offends. She reasoned that if the censorship laws enjoined certain parts of the body from being exposed, "why not a mouth?"

The Stone, a white room made from a transparent paper called shoji, was another component of Ono's "Half-a-Wind Show." By means of a light source outside the room that changed the interior illumination from very dark to very light, the piece emulated the 365-day cycle of the earth as it moves from dawn to dawn. Once inside the room, participants got into black bags. Ono described the experience within the bag as one of self-awareness: "When you are inside the bag, you are observing yourself going from dawn until night, dawn to evening. It is as if you are experiencing a highly abstract life process. . . ."

Accompanying the earlier, collaborative presentation of *The Stone* in March 1966 at the Judson Gallery in New York was Ono's questionnaire, *Truth/False*.

Truth/False

The 6th finger is usually not used because its existence is not physically perceivable. _____

There is a transparent peace tower in New York City which casts no shadow and, therefore, is very rarely recognized. _____

Blood is not red unless exposed, and is blue when it's imagined. _____

The structure of the American jury system is taken from the chance music operation by John Cage. (The noted Judge Connolly is said to have said "all verdicts are beautiful.") _____ (_____)

Mt. Fuji, whose colour is blue and white from the distance and volcano red when you go near, is a carefully planned modern Japanese project built to attract American tourists. _____

The East Side is not a word to define its location but was originally a name of the town "The Wise East on the Wrong Side." Later it was shortened to the presently known "The East Side." _____

Your weight is twice mine, and height 5 inches shorter. _____ _____

Grapefruit is a hybrid of lemon and orange. _____
Snow is a hybrid of wish and lament. _____

All fruits are related species of banana, which was the first fruit in existence. The bible lied about the apple because they felt mentioning the word banana too undignified. _____ _____ _____

Roaches are moving forms of flowers, though visually they seem unconnected. _____

Happenings were first invented by Greek Gods. _____

The word "manila envelope" comes from a deeply-rooted racial prejudice. _____

Coughing is a form of love. _____

All streets are invisible. The visible ones are fake ones, though some visible ones are the end parts of the invisible ones. _____ _____ _____

Teeth and bones are solid forms of cloud. _____

Paper is marble cut so thin that it has become soft. (Make marble out of toilet paper.) _____

Plastic is a portion of sky cut out in solid form. (Collect many pieces of plastic and look through them to see if they look blue.) _____

If you wear a piece of clothing long enough it becomes part of you and you will suffer from serious physical maladjustment when you take it off. A princess died from taking off vines that had covered her for ten years. A prince, when his encircling vines were removed, was found to be non-existent. _____ _____ _____

When you leave things, you leave your spirit behind, too. But if you don't leave them, you age. _____

Your brother is the man you killed in the past world. He was born in your family because he wanted to be near you. _____ _____

There is a wish man in the corner of the world whose daily task is to send good-will waves to the world to clear the air. _____

Men used to walk on hands upside down, but they changed to the present form because it was considered less obscene. _____

What is a circle event?
Do your circle event in the "Stone" pamphlet (50 cents). ad.

99 percent of the world is dead bodies and tombs.
We are the remaining 1 percent . . . . . (or are we?)

There are one thousand suns rising every day. We only see one of them because of our fixation on monistic thinking. _____ _____

Piano keys are flower-petals turned hard. _____

People who bought Ono's "bagwear" invariably encountered fantastic good luck and fortune. –ad.

A cloud consists of the following substances: colour, music, smell, sleep and water. Sometimes it rains substances other than water, but very few people notice it. _____ _____

y.o.

Ono in her "Half-a-Wind Show," Lisson Gallery, London, 1967.

I think of this show as an elephant's tail.

Life is only half a game. Molecules are always at the verge of half disappearing and half emerging.

Somebody said I should also put half-a-person in the show. But we are halves already.

Seng, Sung, Sang, Sing and Song were good musicians. The princess asked them to play for the concert of the midsummer night on the warmest day in Li-Fung. It was a tradition in Li-Fung for the best musicians to get together and play for the people all night and soothe the air from the heat. Seng said he would not play because he did not have enough time to prepare. Sung immediately went into an intensive and elaborate preparation. Sang did nothing. He wandered around the fields until the day came. On the night, Seng was not there. Sung's music overwhelmed people. Sang went on the stage, and when he sung, the warm wind went through his lungs and came out, transformed into the most beautiful music. It was the warm wind that made the music, he said. Sing did not even sing. He just stood on the stage and smiled, and the smile sent vibrations into people's minds, and they heard, they heard their minds tingling, and they smiled back. Do you know anything about Song? People say that he was too pure, and one day, he just suddenly turned into air and was assimilated into the skies.

y.o. excerpts from *Yoko Ono at Lisson*, Lisson Gallery, London, 1967

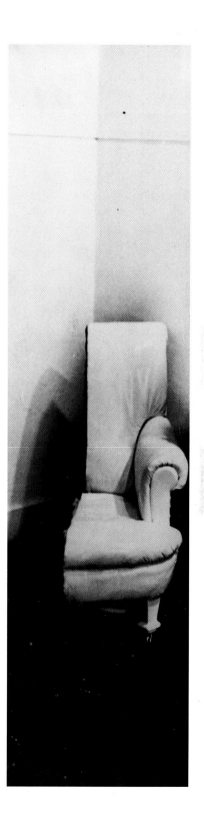

MUSIC OF THE MIND

By 1965, Ono's concerts were billed as "Music of the Mind." By limiting her musical components to the sounds produced in the minds of each audience member, Ono intensified an internal stillness much like that featured in Zen meditation practice.

Ono's concerts in the winter of 1966–67 at the Jeanette Cochrane Theatre (London) and at Bluecoat Chambers (Liverpool) were likewise presented under this rubric. Both programs were sponsored by the Destruction in Art Symposium (DIAS) in which Ono participated that winter. Among the events included in these programs were *Fly Piece,* in which members of the audience came up onstage and jumped off ladders in an effort to simulate flying (see p. 84); a reenactment of *Bag Piece* (see pp. 72-73); and *Sweep Piece,* in which Ono swept the stage from one end to the other.

Wrapping Piece, another inclusion, was performed in the dark; after the audience's eyes adjusted, they perceived the actions in a dim, ethereal light. The piece consisted of performers, wrapped in gauze, being carried onto the stage and placed, one by one, in a heap so that they formed a sculpture. For Ono, the solemn transport of white-clad bodies onto the stage resembled the ritualistic placing of sacred objects on an altar. After all the performers had been carried on stage, Ono illuminated parts of their bodies with a match.

Fog Piece, which closed the program, consisted of Ono, sitting alone onstage, being enveloped in clouds of billowing white vapor—produced by a fog machine—while members of the audience came forward and wrapped her in gauze. By means of a microphone held underneath the gauze, her murmurs of "I am here. Where are you?" could be heard filtering through the smoke. Ono stopped performing the piece after she began to associate it with Egyptian mummification. Whereas other artists might have exploited this overlay, Ono's conviction that life imitates art provoked fear in her, and she stopped performing the piece altogether. "I decided to return the possibility [of mummification] to the metaphysical world and not have anything to do with it."

Poster for Ono's concerts at the Africa Center, London, September 28 and 29, 1966.

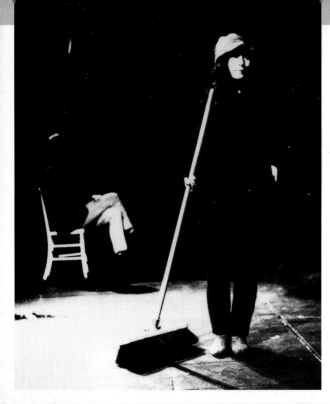

Ono performing *Sweep Piece* at Jeanette Cochrane Theatre, London, 1966.

Ono performing *Shadow Piece* at the Destruction in Art Symposium (DIAS), London, 1966.

Shadow Piece originated as a performance script in 1963: "Put your shadows together until they become one." The idea for the piece was inspired by a short story of a man who lost his shadow. If shadows could be lost, Ono reasoned that they also could be captured. In 1966, she set out to collect the shadows of everyone in the world by tracing the outline of their bodies on one cloth.

Poster for Ono's "Music of the Mind" concert, Bluecoat Chambers, Liverpool, England, 1967.

The High Priestess of the Happening

By GILLIAN LINSCOTT

Miss Yoko Ono—who has spent most of her life puzzling, and occasionally shocking—three continents, hit Liverpool in a cloud of white smoke.

In her Concert of Music for the Mind held at Bluecoat Chambers last Tuesday, she was swathed from head to toe in bandages by volunteers from the audience and then surrounded by clouds of billowing white vapour from a smoke machine.

Inside the cocoon she held a microphone and her murmurs of "I am here. Where are you?" filtered through the smoke to the audience that packed the Bluecoat Chambers to capacity.

Yoko called this Fog Piece and the performance at Liverpool was its world premiere.

Other items in her programme include "Bag Piece" in which she and volunteers from the audience sit on the stage completely enclosed in bags, and "Fly Piece" an invitation to members of the audience to try to fly from the top of 20-foot stepladders.

Some people would call it madness and Yoko would hardly resent the description. She confessed that she always feels closer to the borderline of what is usually thought of as sanity.

But the ideas behind her performances are far from insane, as the students of the Liverpool College of Art found when Yoko lectured to them on Wednesday.

When the audience are the show

Audience reaction is the key point to Ono's concerts. When she sits in silence on the stage, peering at the audience through a slit in a box, she is trying to make them think about themselves by reversing the usual theatre situation, making the watchers the watched.

She hopes, she says, that this will make them more conscious of people and things around them, more free for using their imagination.

"I want people to see imaginary colours, hear imaginary music," she says. "There are never any sounds at my concerts because the real music is in people's minds."

The claims she makes for her concerts are like those that the hippies make for L.S.D., but Yoko believes that heightened awareness can be achieved without using drugs.

She was enthusiastic about the Liverpool atmosphere. "London is good, but its approach to my work is more intellectual, wanting to know reasons for things. The audience here was wonderful, very responsive —beautiful young people."

One of her recent experiments in communication was less successful. She made a film consisting entirely of pictures of 365 bare bottoms which was refused a licence for public showing. She thinks that the publicity resulting from this might have attracted to her Liverpool concert, some people who would not otherwise have come, but if they expected an evening of erotic pictures—or any erotic pictures at all—they were disappointed.

The match that started it all

How did Yoko begin on her strange concerts. She thinks that her parents' religion might have had something to do with it.

"My mother was a Buddhist and my father Christian. I was born in Tokio. From the age of five I learnt music and composing, because my father wanted me to become a concert pianist.

"Then later I studied philosophy—the usual range, existentialism, zen Buddhism, but none of them had the whole answer."

Still a student in Tokio she tried to work out an answer for herself. She says that her ideas on helping people to communicate began with a match flame.

"I lit a match and watched it burn—just that."

For fifteen years since then, in Japan, America and England she has been working out a stage programme that is the equivalent of the burning match—ordinary events presented in extraordinary ways to make people think about them for the first time.

She came to England, she said, because she felt that in America she was becoming part of a particular group of people, and that made communication difficult.

Where would she go if that happened in England? "I don't know," she said. "I never make plans. Things just happen."

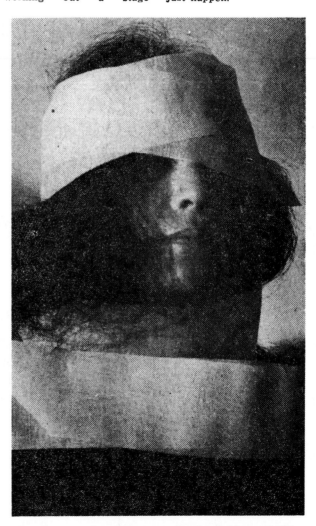

Yoko Ono, in bandages, at the beginning of "Fog Piece" at her Bluecoat Chambers concert.

Gillian Linscott, "The High Priestess of the Happening," *Liverpool Daily Post*, March 10, 1967 (excerpt).

Lennon and Ono performing *Silent Piece*, 1972.

In 1972, Ono and John Lennon performed a variant of Ono's "Music of the Mind" at the memorial concert for Ken Dewey in Elysian Meadows. For this event, Lennon strummed an imaginary guitar while Ono silently screamed into a microphone. The music was thus intangible—an internalization that seemed appropriate for a memorial tribute.

LINGUISTIC PARADOX

Language is a central component of Ono's art, whether in performance and film scripts or in two- and three-dimensional objects. In some works, the provocative obscurity of the texts themselves suggest a world unbounded by the normal constrictions of time and space. In others, the juxtaposition of text and object create paradoxical conundrums intended to trigger nonrational ways of thinking.

Pointedness, 1988 (bronze version of 1964 work)
"This sphere will be a sharp point when it gets to the far corners of the room in your mind."   y.o.

Pointedness evolved from Ono's appreciation of the scientific hypothesis that space is not straight but curved. Her implicit suggestion that spheres and points may be different manifestations of the same phenomenon extended this proposition. Beyond the poetic paradox created by such an extension lies Ono's fundamental belief in the legitimacy of different, but equally valid, interpretations of the conditions of the world.

I think it is possible to see a chair as it is. But when you burn the chair, you suddenly realize that the chair in your head did not burn or disappear. . . .

Isn't a construction a beginning of a thing like a seed? Isn't it a segment of a larger totality, like an elephant's tail? Isn't it something just about to emerge—not quite structured—never quite structured . . . like an unfinished church with a sky ceiling? . . .

———————————————————   ———————————————————

A marble sphere (actually existing) which, in your head, gradually becomes a sharp cone by the time it is extended to the far end of the room.

A garden covered with thick marble instead of snow—but like snow, which is to be appreciated only when you uncover the marble coating.

One thousand needles: imagine threading them with a straight thread.

Excerpts from Ono's *To the Wesleyan People,* 1966

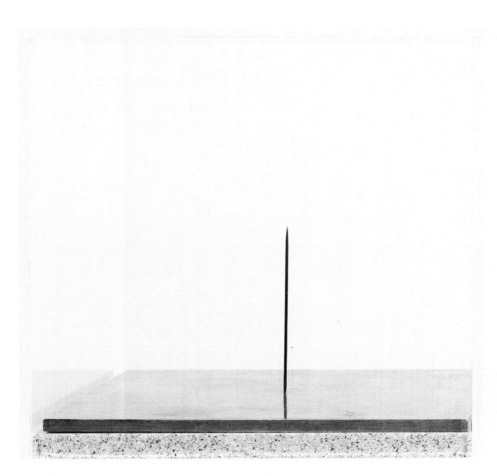

Forget It, 1988 (bronze version of 1966 work)

Forget It materialized Ono's association of needles with psychological pain. "When someone says something hurtful, I always perceive it as a needle being stabbed into me." The title's admonition to "forget it" is a reminder of the necessity of moving into the future without the psychological baggage of the past. At the same time, the title paradoxically calls forth its opposite: the very attempt to forget a specific experience often implants it more fully into our memory. By refocusing on it, we initiate a dialogue between it and our desire to forget it.

There's no ownership in beauty.   y.o. from *Museum of Modern (F)art*, December, 1971

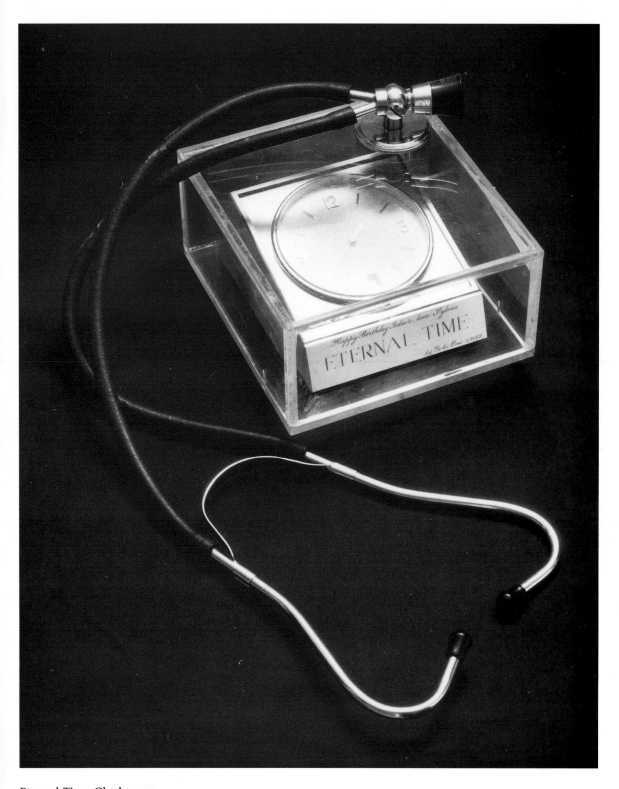

Eternal Time Clock, 1965

Eternal Time Clock was commissioned as a birthday present for a friend's husband. To create the piece, Ono removed the minute and hour hands from an open-faced clock, leaving only the second hand. Thus, time passed but could not be measured. Ono's title suggested that eternity is similarly time-*less*—a continuum in which there is no past and future. As if eternal time was something one could listen to rather than see, Ono attached a stethoscope to her *Eternal Time Clock*.

Mailing Piece I   Send a sound of a smile.   y.o. 1962 summer

A Box of Smile, 1967

A Box of Smile contains a mirror on its inside lid which reflects the smile of whoever opens the box. While the title of the piece can be interpreted as referring to this smile, it can simultaneously be viewed as implying that the box is full of smiles. In this latter reading, Ono seems to be proposing that physically immaterial entities—like smiles—are experienced as palpable despite their absence of concrete materiality. In her texts on ownership, she reflects on the implications of such immateriality.

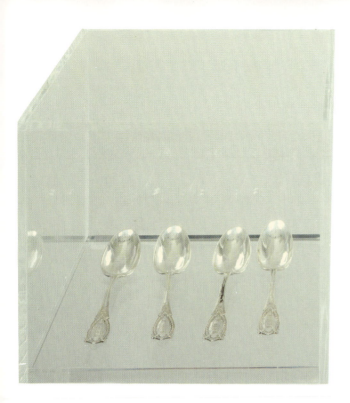

Three Spoons, 1967
The Gilbert and Lila Silverman Fluxus Collection Foundation

Consisting, as it did, of four spoons, *Three Spoons* set up a disjunction between language and factual reality. John Lennon responded to this playful contradiction of visible reality with a more literal version of the piece called *Four Spoons,* which contained four spoons. "Realism," as he stated in 1969, "leaves a lot to the imagination."

To Be Appreciated Only When It's Broken, 1988 (bronze version of 1967 work)

Disappearing Piece

Boil water.

This piece was first performed in New York, 1966, by only five people. This was not deliberate, but probably due to the subway strike in New York at the time. The water was boiled in a still, until it came out on the other side of the still, which took two hours. In London, 1966, Mercury Theatre, the boiling of the water, the size of the pot in which the water was boiled, etc., was announced on stage. The actual boiling of the water was performed at a Notting Hill Gate flat. The complete evaporation of the water was announced from the stage as the ending of the piece.

y.o.

Disappearing Piece, 1988 (bronze version of 1965 work)
The object in this box will disappear when the lid is opened.   y.o.

Disappearing Piece likewise suggests the existence of entities or states of mind which elude material verification. As Ono noted, "The world of construction seems to be the most tangible, and therefore final. This made me nervous. I started to wonder if it were really so."

On Ownership I

Once there was a warrior who visited a farmer and asked if he could buy an old cherry-tree in the farmer's back yard. The farmer agreed to sell, and a reasonable amount of gold was paid for it. The farmer then asked if the warrior wanted to have the cherry-tree delivered somewhere. The warrior said that he had no intention of moving the poor cherry-tree. He just wanted to come when it blossomed and sit beneath the tree to appreciate it. "Well, then, you don't have to pay for that!" the farmer cried. "I'll let you come and sit beneath the cherry-tree when it blossoms!" "You don't seem to understand," the warrior said with a smile. "Unless I know that I own it, I can't enjoy it."

y.o. from *Museum of Modern (F)art*, December, 1971

Omnibus Film
(unrealized film script)

1) Give a print of the same film to many directors.
2) Ask each one to re-edit the print without leaving out any of the material in such a way that it will be unnoticed that the print was re-edited.
3) Show all the versions together omnibus style.

y.o. 1964

On Ownership II

1) An evening light was shining on Empire State Blg.
2) Mary pointed out to Bob that the evening light was shining on Empire State Blg.
3) Bob took a photo of the evening light shining on Empire State Blg. and sent it to Jim.
4) Jim wrote a song about the evening light shining on Empire State Blg. and made a record.
5) Liz bought the record and listened to the song on the evening light shining on Empire State Blg. She cried.

The evening light on Empire State Blg. was passed around among four people.
Pass around something else.
Pass around an apple.
What happens?

Pass around money.
What happens?
When you pass around, if you decide to keep it instead, do you own the money?

Pass around evening light again. Then try to keep the evening light. Do you own the evening light?

What happens when you don't pass around things? Try it with ice-cream, a secret, and love.

What happens when you eat things and you decide to keep them in your body and not pass them out?

What happens when your body gets clogged?
What happens when your mind gets clogged?

Count all the things you've kept instead of passing it around.

y.o. from *Museum of Modern (F)art*, December, 1971

Chewing Gum Machine Piece

Place Chewing Gum Machines with many
 different word cards in them next to
 Coca-Cola Machines on every
 street corner.
Make it so that a word card comes out
 when you put one cent in.
Put more auxiliary words than nouns.
More verbs than adjectives.

y.o. 1961 winter

Air Dispenser, 1971

Air Dispenser was one of a number of dispensers which Ono created for her Everson Museum exhibition in 1971. Containing capsules filled with air which sold for twenty-five cents apiece, *Air Dispenser* addressed the absurdity of attempting to contain or own intangible natural phenomenon.

SKY AND CLOUDS

Sky and clouds, symbols to Ono of unbridled freedom and boundlessness, are frequent subjects in her work. In treating them as her focus, Ono conjoined vanguard techniques with an Oriental regard for the evanescence and delicacy of nature. As Ono's writings make clear, mutable natural elements such as clouds and skies are incapable of being possessed—or owned. By treating them as if they were solid, concrete substances, Ono suggests an alternate—and poetic—interpretation to normative assumptions about reality.

Film still from *Apotheosis*, 1970. Produced and directed in collaboration with John Lennon.

Cloud Piece

Imagine the clouds dripping.
Dig a hole in your garden to
put them in.

y.o. 1963 spring

Lennon and Ono in a production photograph from *Apotheosis*, 1969

As an analogue to Ono's earlier instruction piece, which directed viewers to "Cut along dotted line and look at the sky through the hole," the camera lens in *Apotheosis* became the opening through which viewers focused on an isolated perception. As with Ono's other images of sky and clouds, the ascent of the balloon above the English countryside was a metaphor for the freedom she and Lennon sought in their lives and art.

Sky Event for John Lennon

The organizer of the event may select one version from the following:

a] wait until a cloud appears and come above your head
b] wait until the snow falls
c] wait until a chair falls

All three versions can be done in any season of the year. People should gather with their Sunday outfit, wearing their best hats, etc.

If the weather is cold, burn fire, if it is warm pass cold drinks and wait.

Stop cars and people on the street and inform them of the event that's taking place. Let them join. Call friends and strangers on the phone and ask them to join.

Prepare binoculars and telescopes for people to occasionally check the sky. Ladders of great height should be prepared for people who wish to climb up high to check.

The gathering can take place both outside and indoors. If it's indoor, it will be nice to gather in a room with a large window. If it's a closed room, take turns to go out and check.

Take photographs of the sky, the town and the people, before, during and after the wait.

Do not talk loud or make noise, as you may scare the sky.

y.o. 1968 spring

Sky Event II
(Imaginary Sky Event—refer to Sky Event for John Lennon)

Do the Sky Event in your mind.
THEN Go out into the street and take photos to document the event

If the sky event in your mind takes place in another city, ask a friend in that city to take photos for you.

y.o. 1968

Painting to See the Skies

Drill two holes into a canvas.
Hang it where you can see the sky.

(Change the place of hanging.
Try both the front and the rear windows,
to see if the skies are different.)

y.o. 1961 summer

A Painting to See the Sky III

See the sky between a woman's thighs.
See the sky between your own thighs.
See the sky through your belongings by making holes in them.

i.e.: pants, jacket, shirt, stockings, etc.

y.o. 1962 autumn

Sky People

I stopped flying a long time ago
Thinking that's just for the birds and the
    bees
But when I look up and see the sky
I like the blue and I know why

You come from Zeus, we come from
    Uranus
Hoping to meet soul to soul
We see you clearly with our third eye
There's no more fear and I know why

'Cause we're sky people that's what we are
Sky people that's what we are
One day we'll fly and leap through the sky
To look for the good land hand in hand

(You know who sky people are
They've got the blues in what they wear)

       y.o. 1985; song included in *Starpeace*

John Lennon as a Young Cloud

Theatre Piece

scene 1) Open and close inside John's
    head.
scene 2) Open and close other people's
    head.
scene 3) Open and close sky.

       y.o. 1968 spring

Film No. 11
Passing
(unrealized film script)

See the sky from the bottom of a very
    deep well.

A cloud passes through slowly
From left to right and disappears.

       y.o. 1968

Tape Piece IV
Moving Piece

Take a tape of the sound of the stars
    moving.
Do not listen to the tape.
Cut it and give it out to the people on the
    street.
Or you may sell it for a moderate price.

       y.o. 1963 autumn

ENTER: SKY ➡
silently.
open and close all the doors in the flat.
watch the dawn.

       y.o. 1966

Sky No. 1 (Key to Open the Skies), 1967

Front album cover of *The Plastic Ono Band—Live Peace in Toronto,* 1969

Film No. 10
Sky

It is a film about waiting.

First you see the sky through a telescope that covers the whole screen. The effect is like seeing the sky from the bottom of a very deep well. Clouds pass through very slowly.

Four people all dressed up are on a top of the hill.
They are watching the sky.
And waiting, and waiting.

Some small talk between the four (all improvised).

Then one suggests that he would bring something and goes off.
Remaining three talk about the one who went off.
Then the third one goes off
Remaining two talk about the two who went off.

Then the third one goes off.
Remaining one moves around by himself. Then goes off.

The first one comes back with an incense.
The second and third ones comes back, too.
But they can't find any matches between them to light the incense.

One goes off to get matches.
Another one goes off to get something.
The remaining one lies down to take a nap.
(notice that the fourth one never came back)

Matches are brought back.
The second one brings back a guitar.

He starts to play and three of them sing.
Then they decide that the singing might scare the "thing" away, so they stop singing.

(constant looking up at the sky and horizon)

Then one suggests that somebody should bring a big ladder.
There is a discussion about who should bring the ladder.
They draw straws and the one who got the shortest goes off.

Then he comes back and says he needs another one to help him bring it. So finally all three of them go together.

Then the three bring back a ladder—a huge ladder.
Two hold the bottom and one goes up and looks at the sky with a huge telescope.

Still nothing.

Gradually, it gets dark and they use matches to see each other's faces.
It gets cold and they make fire.
Also, one person gets extremely cold, so the rest of them give all their coats.

Finally, they see the fourth guy, who was away all this time, come back.

"Have you guys seen it yet?"
"No, not yet."

They are still checking the sky.
Suddenly one says "look, look!"
Everybody looks.

"Did you see it?"
"No."
"Maybe"
". . .?"

They put out the fire they made, which was getting low anyway.
And they go off with the ladder, telescope and each other.

y.o. 1968

I would like to see the sky machine on every corner of the street instead of the coke machine. We need more skies than coke.

y.o.

Sky Machine, 1965
The Gilbert and Lila Silverman Fluxus Collection Foundation

Sky Machine offered a variation on Ono's paradoxical concretizing of immaterial substances. In this piece, she played with the relationship between an object and its language equivalent—between the signifier and the signified. When viewers put money into the designated slot, they received a piece of paper hand-written with the word "sky."

On Sky

How could you let the fly fly, and don't you fly at all?

That's because you have the notion that the sky starts there up high.
If you knew that in actual fact that the sky starts under your feet,
It won't be too much of a problem for you to fly with the fly or a pie.

y.o. from *Museum of Modern (F)art*, December 1971

A Shovel to Dig a Hole for the Clouds to Drop In, 1971

CAMOUFLAGE

Ono's wrapping pieces, which deal with the idea of concealment and revelation, manifest her view that the reality we perceive is approximate and incomplete—that it is "only part of the big reality."

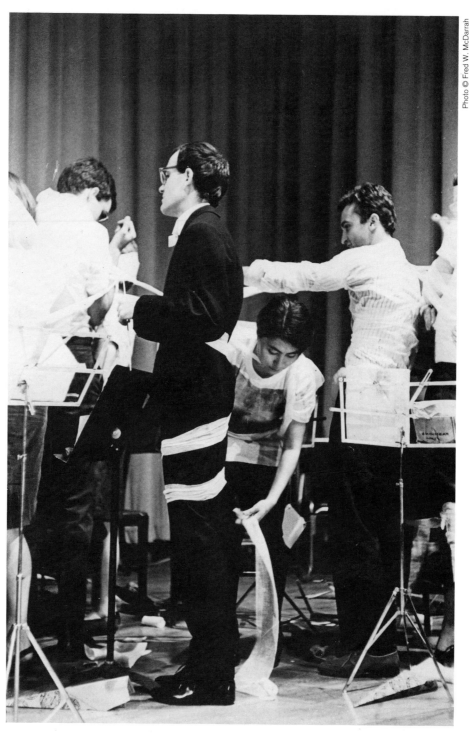

Ono performing *Sky Piece for Jesus Christ* with the Fluxorchestra at Carnegie Recital Hall, New York, 1965

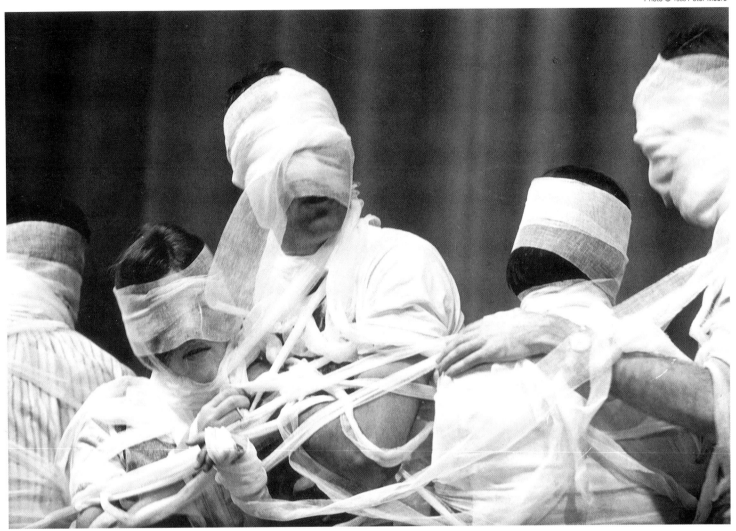

Sky Piece for Jesus Christ, with the Fluxorchestra at Carnegie Recital Hall, New York, 1965

In *Sky Piece for Jesus Christ,* Ono transformed the musicians on stage by wrapping them in gauze. As each musician was bound, his instrument died out until, finally, all were quiet. Ono then wrapped the musicians into one unit—an act which prevented them from playing, while also insuring that they moved together as one entity. For Ono, the group effort that was demanded of the musicians as they exited offstage was a model for an idealized state of interdependence which her title implicitly equates with Christianity.

Ono believed that all realities imply—indeed even contain—their opposite. "Our imaginations embrace what we do not have or cannot be," Ono remarked. "Someone in prison does not think about anything but the sky. . . . They do not think about the prison—they think about the nightlife in New York. . . . The reason people get so enticed by the sky and think so much about it is due to the restrictions surrounding their lives." Ono even goes so far as to argue that the human capacity to imagine opposite states accounts for the pervasive hold religion has on people's imaginations; despite the bounded, repressive conditions in which individuals live, an unbounded reality can be imagined. As in this piece, the physical restrictions imposed on the performers called to mind images of freedom—associated in Ono's mind with sky. "It is almost as if you can visualize the sky because the performers' difficulties in walking is so opposite to the freedom that the sky represents."

Bag Piece

After the curtain has gone up (or if there is no curtain, at a designated time after the announcer announces the piece) two performers walk onto the stage.

Performers may be two males, two females, or a mixed couple.
Performers carry a bag large enough for both to get inside of.
Bag made of non-transparent material.
Both performers get inside of bag.
Both remove all clothing while inside of bag.
Both put all clothing back on.
They come out of bag.
They exit with bag from stage.

y.o.

First presented in Tokyo and New York in 1962 and 1965 respectively, *Bag Piece* was also included in Ono's "Music of the Mind" concert in London. The piece consisted of Yoko and an assistant crawling into a huge black bag, undressing, redressing, and then exiting. Since the actions performed within the bag remained mysterious to the audience, the common assumption was that something sexual had taken place within the bag.

For Ono, *Bag Piece* addressed the issue of who we are, how we know who we are, and how we communicate this knowledge to others. "If we were not to have the shape we have," Ono asks, "would we still be ourselves?" For Ono, the answer is affirmative. Furthermore, she believes that masking external appearance forces a more direct understanding of reality and of our incomplete view of it. According to her, we live our lives as if in a bag: "When you are in the bag, you can see outside. But when you are outside, you can only see the outline of the bag. It is very easy for us to clearly see outside and say 'listen. I'm here—you can see what I am.' But, of course, the other person can only see your outline." Yet, however false or misleading this approximation is, it does not alter our essence. As Ono says, "When we hide what we consider to be all the exterior aspects of ourselves . . . we are still who we are."

Ono and Tony Cox performing *Bag Piece* at the Africa Center, London, 1966

Wrapping Event, Trafalgar Square, London, 1967

The Trafalgar Square *Wrapping Event* grew out of the wrapped chair in Ono's Indica Gallery exhibition. The scale of the objects to be wrapped differed, but the effect and content did not; as with the chair, Ono's wrapping of the lions in Trafalgar Square simultaneously concealed and revealed their forms. Ono's initial attempt to cover the lions with gauze and toilet paper failed. She realized that "it would have taken ages to wrap them up." She returned to the site in August 1967 with large pieces of fabric. *Wrapping Event,* intended as both an event and a film, helped insure Ono's growing fame in London as a leading member of the vanguard art community.

For her exhibition at the Indica Gallery, London, Ono placed a roll of gauze on a chair with the intention that viewers would decorate the gallery with streams of the material. Instead, they wrapped the chair.

The wrapped chair was re-presented in Ono's one-person exhibition at the Everson Museum in 1971 with the addition of a transparent plexiglass enclosure and the paradoxical title, *Hide Me*. This version of the piece reversed normal expectations; the plexiglass box, presumably intended to "hide" or protect the piece, actually served to draw more attention to it. For Ono, this had autobiographical implications; the more she attempted to hide, the more she revealed herself. Indeed, she came to believe that hiding—represented by the wrapped chair—can never be successful; the underlying character of the self can never be fully camouflaged. Like other of Ono's wrapped work, these two versions of the wrapped chair explored the question of who we are: are we the body that one usually sees or are we something else?

Wrapping Piece for London (before wrapping), 1966

PAINTINGS TO COMPL

Rearrangement Piece, 1966

As with Ono's *Painting to Be Constructed in Your Head,* the individual elements in Ono's rearrangement pieces could actually be arranged by viewers or simply configured in their minds. In either case, the execution strategy allowed for audience participation and chance as well as change and metamorphosis.

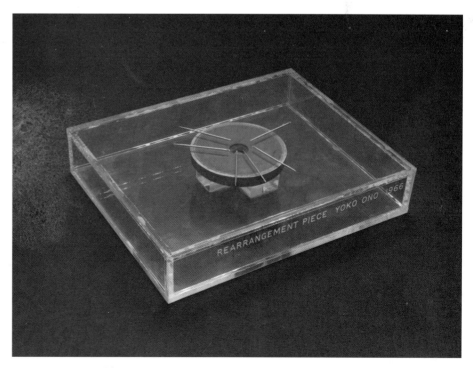

Rearrangement Piece, 1966

ETE IN THE MIND

Painting to Be Constructed in Your Head

Observe three paintings carefully.
Mix them well in your head.

y.o. 1962 spring

Mend Painting, 1966

Painting to Be Constructed in Your Head

Imagine dividing the canvas into twenty different shapes. Make the exact model of each piece and send it to an address arbitrarily chosen. Write the twenty addresses and the corresponding shapes of the pieces on the back of the canvas.

y.o. 1962 spring

Painting to Be Constructed in Your Head

Hammer a nail in the center of a piece of glass. Imagine sending the cracked portions to addresses chosen arbitrarily. Memo the addresses and the shapes of the cracked portions sent.

y.o. 1962 spring

Mending Piece I, 1966

Mending Piece I, with its broken cup, glue, needle and thread, was presented as a sculpture in Ono's Indica Gallery show. The act of mending the sculpture was to occur in people's minds—a conceptual strategy which recalled Ono's 1961 "part paintings," whose pieces had been scattered around the rooms of the AG Gallery and were likewise to be reconstituted in the minds of the viewers.

In the initial performance version, entitled *Promise Piece* (1966), Ono broke a vase on the stage and asked people to pick up the pieces and take them home, promising that they would reunite in ten years and mend the vase. Ono's intention was to manifest the community participation that is required in order to rebuild—even when the rebuilding takes place over time.

Part Painting
Series 5

congratulations!

you are one of the 10,000 selected people to whom we are sending this part painting by yoko ono. each person has received a portion of this painting. we are planning to hold a gathering in the future to put all parts together to appreciate the painting in its original form. but meanwhile, you may recommend [to] us select names to send parts as there are a few still in our hand[s]. it is important that you mention in your letter the social position of your friend, as the size of the portion will be decided accordingly.

y.o.

Vase Piece, performed by Ono in her Everson Museum retrospective, 1971 (reenactment of *Promise Piece*, 1966).

EQUIVALENCE

Balance Piece, 1966
Leave your fingernails to balance these scales.   y.o.

Many of Ono's works addressed the fundamental parity that exists between substances whose outward form and material qualities differ. Reality, Ono believed, was interchangeable when considered from a molecular level. In her film script *Travelogue,* she eradicated specificity and context by radically cropping landscape images. By treating these deracinated images as the repository of memories of a trip, Ono parodied the traditional travel film. Conceptually, the film echoed her series of part paintings from 1971 in which she cropped and magnified a portion of an object, thereby rendering it unidentifiable and hence abstract.

The Connection

Once we were fish
moving freely in the sea.
Our bodies were soft and swift
and we had no belongings.

Now that we crawled out of the sea
we are dry and full of cravings.
We wander city to city
carrying the memory of the sea
(but it isn't just a memory.)

Listen very carefully and you will hear
the sea in your body.
You know, our blood is seawater
and we are all seacarriers.

From Ono's *Seven Little Stories;* originally in Japanese

You and Me, 1966

"When we were fish," Ono wrote in 1967 for her Lisson Gallery catalogue, "the sea-water surrounded us. When we came on ground, we carried the sea inside us. Our blood structure is 90% salt-water." By filling two condoms with water, Ono underscores the commonality of people, all of whose bodies are composed primarily of water.

Water Talk

you are water
I'm water
we're all water in different containers
that's why it's so easy to meet
someday we'll evaporate together

but even after the water's gone
we'll probably point out to the containers
and say, "that's me there, that one"
we're container minders

y.o. 1967

Water Piece, 1966 (reconstruction of a 1962 work)

We're All Water

There may be not much difference
Between Chairman Mao and Richard Nixon
If we strip them naked.

There may be not much difference
Between Marilyn Monroe and Lenny Bruce
If we check their coffins.

There may be not much difference
Between White House and Hall of People
If we count their windows.

There may be not much difference
Between Raquel Welch and Jerry Rubin
If we hear their heartbeat.

Chorus:
We're all water from different rivers
That's why it's so easy to meet
We're all water in this vast, vast ocean
Someday we'll evaporate together.

There may be not much difference
Between Eldridge Cleaver and Queen of
    England
If we bottle their tears.

There may be not much difference
Between Manson and the Pope
If we press their smile.

There may be not much difference
Between Rockefeller and you
If we hear you sing.

There may be not much difference
Between you and me
If we show our dreams.

y.o. 1972; song included in *Some Time in New York City*

FLYING

Fly Piece

Fly.

        y.o. 1963 summer

Fly Piece, Kyoto, 1964

Fly Piece, Kyoto, 1964

Fly Piece was performed in Ono's "Music of the Mind" concerts—in Kyoto (1964) and England (1967–68)—by audience members who came up on the stage and jumped off the ladders that Ono had prepared for them. Ono associated this act of simulated flying with freedom as well as with the obverse of flying—falling. "The interesting thing about flying is that the time when you are flying is always followed by a time when you are going to land." For Ono, this dual aspect manifested the symbiosis that informs all aspects of reality.

How to Fly

1) Make sure that your mind is not clogged with heavy burdens such as: resentment, anger, secrets and the past. They can be heavy.

2) Make sure that your body is not clogged with excess fat and excrements.

3) Make sure that your wings are light and free. This is the most difficult proposition. Your wings cannot be free unless the whole world is free, because you are part of the world. However, there is a way for the whole world to be free. Just like your body, all it needs is to be unclogged and have good circulation. Circulation is the secret to freedom and the key to fly.

5) When the whole world is in good circulation we will all fly together.

6) Meanwhile, give wings to things around you so they will circulate.

y.o. from *Museum of Modern (F)art,* December, 1971

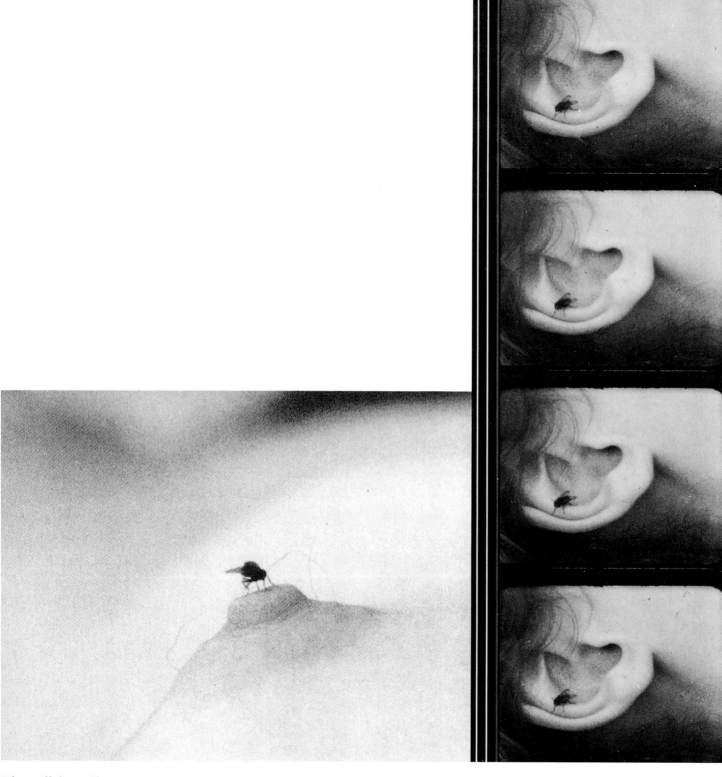

Film still from *Fly*, 1970

Filmstrip from *Fly*, 1970

In 1970 Ono completed one of her best-known films, the 24-minute *Fly*, in which we follow a fly as it moves about a nude female body. The contours of the human body became an extraordinary landscape, at once familiar and bizarre. As the camera moves over the details of this landscape, Ono's accompanying vocal inflections appear to inhabit the fly.

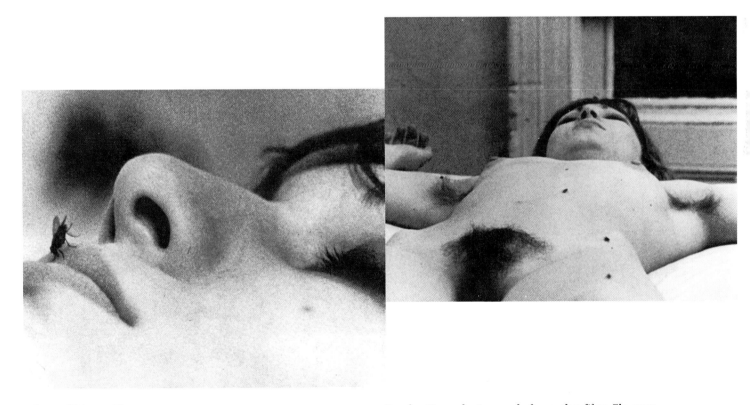

Film still from *Fly*, 1970

Production photograph from the film *Fly*, 1970.

Film No. 13
Fly

87   Let a fly walk on a woman's body from toe to head and fly out of the window.   y.o. 1968

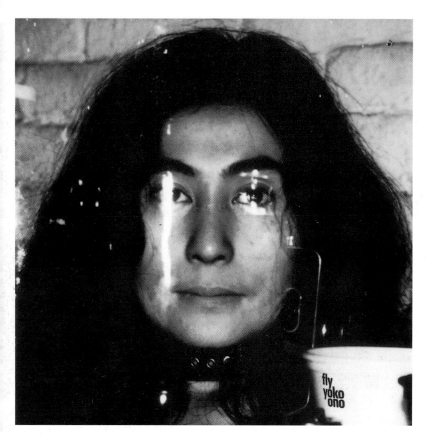

Front cover of Ono's album *Fly*, 1971

Song for John

On a windy day
Let's go on flying
There may be no trees to rest on
There may be no clouds to ride
But we'll have our wings
And the wind will be with us
That's enough for me
That's enough for me

On a windy day
We went on flying
There was no sea to rest on
There were no hills to glide
We saw an empty bottle rolling down the street
And on a cardboard stand at the corner of the street
Wrinkled souls
Piled up
Like grapefruits

y.o. 1973; song included in *Approximately Infinite Universe*

Flies and flying were the ostensible subjects of the one-woman exhibition which Ono organized for herself, without the institution's knowledge, at The Museum of Modern Art, New York, in December 1971. The only indication that the exhibition was occurring was a descriptive placard, written by Ono, which was carried by a sandwich man in front of the museum.

Two pages from Ono's catalogue *The Museum of Modern (F)art*, 1971

For the event, Ono supposedly filled a glass container with flies. She placed the container, equal in volume to her body and sponged with the perfume she typically used, in the exact center of the museum's garden and opened the lid. Participants in the event were invited to join the artist and her photographer in following the flies around the city to determine how far the flies flew and where they landed—a task presumably made possible by the distinguishing odor of the flies.

The placard announcing the exhibition seemed so authoritative that visitors to the museum assumed the show was genuine. Museum officials were forced to put up notification at the entrance to the ticket booth that Ono's show was not being held there.

The film *The Museum of Modern Art Show* (1971) documents visitors to the museum who are being questioned about the idea of a Yoko Ono show at the institution.

FEMINISM: VIOLENCE

Running through much of Ono's work is a bold commentary on women. Yet far from being strident feminist tracts on the subordination and victimization of women, her pieces achieve power because of their ambiguity; their willingness to forfeit the illusion of politically proper thinking throws responsibility for judgment upon the viewer.

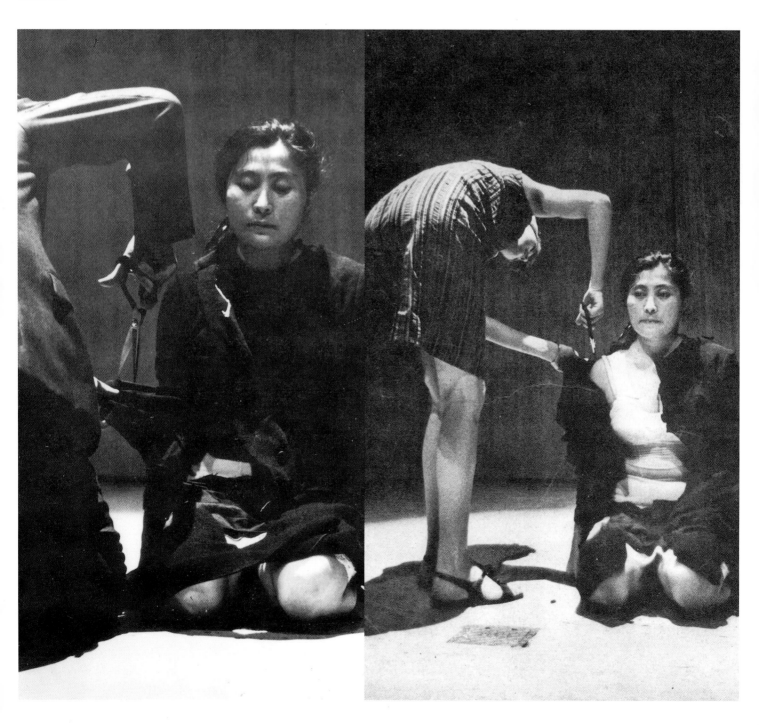

Ono performing *Cut Piece* at the Yamaichi Concert Hall, Kyoto, Japan, 1964.

AND LIBERATION

Cut Piece premiered in Kyoto, Japan, at the Yamaichi Concert Hall in 1964 and in New York at Carnegie Recital Hall in 1965. As described by a contemporary critic, the Carnegie Recital Hall concert consisted of Ono, wearing an expensive suit, sitting on stage and inviting members of the audience to come up and cut off her clothing. "As one by one, men and women snipped off more and more of her suit and underclothing the tension mounted. An adolescent boy came up and amputated her bra, by which point most of the audience were possessed by fear and anxiety and realized they were trapped by the piece." At the first Kyoto performance, latent violence nearly erupted. As Ono described it, "One person came on the stage…. He took the pair of scissors and made a motion to stab me. He raised his hand, with the scissors in it, and I thought he was going to stab me. But the hand was just raised there and was totally still. He was standing still … with the scissors, … threatening me."

Cut Piece drew inspiration from an allegorical story of the Buddha which Ono heard often as a child. According to legend, Buddha renounced his privileged position to go out into the world and to give whatever was requested of him. At the moment when he allowed a tiger to eat his body, Buddha's soul entered the realm of supreme awareness. The relationship between the Buddha's giving and the artist's giving intrigued Ono. By allowing the audience to cut off her clothes, she attempted to symbolize the artist's giving. She always wore her best suit when performing the piece, on the theory that if you give an offering, you give the best. At the first performance of the piece in Japan, a mood of reverence prevailed. "It was very, very difficult for people to come up. So there would be very long silences and then you would hear the scissors cutting. There were quiet and beautiful silences — quiet and beautiful movements." The same feeling of piety prevailed in a performance which Charlotte Moorman gave in a nunnery. For Ono, the nuns' apparent understanding of the piece and their sense that it represented what they were doing with their own lives vindicated her belief in the parallelism of religion and the avant-garde.

Yet *Cut Piece* did not exclusively affirm the Buddhist ideal of selflessness, but dealt also with questions of violence and personal violation. By overtly enacting the sexually submissive role with which females traditionally have been associated, Ono forces the audience to confront their own attitudes toward sexual aggression, voyeurism, and gender subordination. In most performances these questions elicited an aura of discomfort. The psychological effectiveness of the piece owed to the position of vulnerability which Ono assumed while onstage.

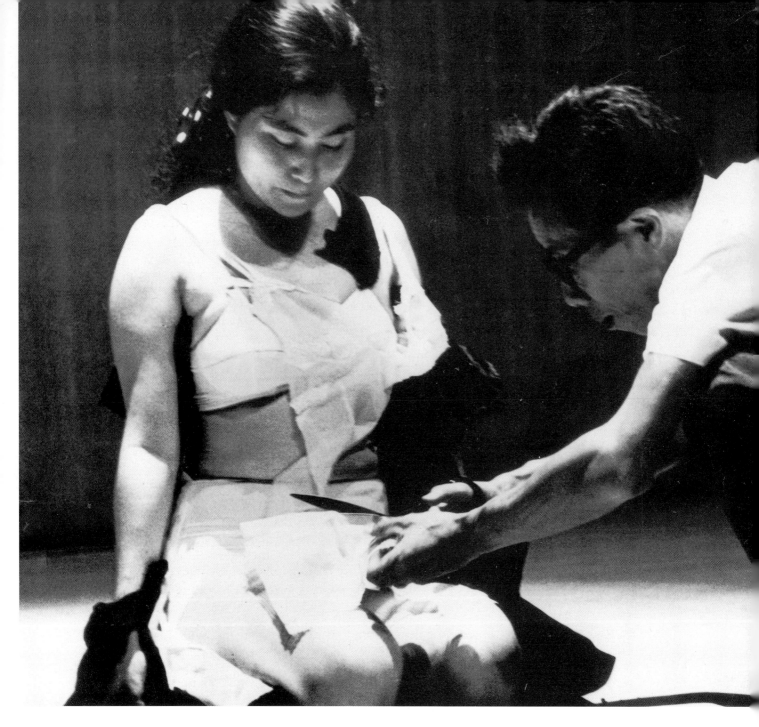

Cut Piece

First version for single performer:

Performer sits on stage with pair of scissors placed in front of him.
It is announced that members of the audience may come on stage — one at a time — to cut a small piece of the performer's clothing to take with them.
Performer remains motionless throughout the piece.
Piece ends at the performer's option.

Second version for audience:
It is announced that members of the audience may cut each others clothing.
The audience may cut as long as they want.

y.o.

Film No. 8 (Woman)

1-1/2 hour. Color. Separate soundtrack. Cast: one woman.

This is a film about pregnancy and delivery treated in a highly poetic way, as opposed to a medical report sort.

The pregnant woman is the only person in the entire film, which symbolizes the lonely venture of conception.

She is contemporary, very sensitive and intelligent. Her mentality in all phases of her thinking is equivalent to that of a man of high intelligence in our society.

The audience becomes intimate with her skin, her swell, her vomit, her walk, her smile, everything about her except her exterior circumstances, such as whether she is married, if she has a job, etc. That part of her background is completely obscure.

The whole film can be thought of as a solo dance movement of a pregnant woman: first very light and pretty—gradually the body protruding—heavy and slow, and finally the dramatic delivery and a complete stillness to follow, with an underlying suggestion of peace/death (atonement).

We also see a lot of the town, the skies the stars through her pregnant eyes.

In the soundtrack, we go into her mind. It consists mostly of delivery groans, swearing, also interviews of the woman done by imaginary reporters. The quality of the interviews are highly philosophic—something that can be compared to the last monologue in *L'etranger* by Camus. She first conceives of her experience as a cancer growing in her stomach, etc. She is committed. But why her and not the man? What is the relationship between her and the growth inside her? etc., etc.

Except for medical reports, no film-maker as yet has taken this subject for a film. Maybe it is because most film-makers are men and they are sensitive to this subject. I have noticed that whenever a pregnant woman is shown in a photograph or a film, they are over beautified and romanticized with careful camera work.

I want to treat this film poetically, but not with unnecessary beautification.

I want all the girls in the world to see the film before they become pregnant. Some mothers, because they have been wrongly informed that the pregnancy is the most gratifying thing for women, etc., they start to hate the child after the initial shock of going through the unglamorous reality of pregnancy.

I want to eliminate such tragedy in the world.

Financially, this is a film that can be made with minimum cost. Though it takes time to make it (6 months) and today, most film-makers would like to spend less time in making a film, I don't mind going through it, since I feel this is a very important film.

y.o. 1968

Film Script No. 5
Rape (or Chase)

Rape with camera. 1-1/2 hour color synchronized sound.

A cameraman will chase a girl on a street with a camera persistently until he corners her in an alley, and, if possible, until she is in a falling position.

The cameraman will be taking a risk of offending the girl as the girl is somebody he picks up arbitrarily on the street, but there is a way to get around this.

Depending on the budget, the chase should be made with girls of different age, etc. May chase boys and men as well.

As the film progresses, and as it goes towards the end, the chase and the running should become slower and slower like in a dream, using a highspeed camera.

y.o. 1968

Film still from *Rape*, 1969.

On Rape

Violence is a sad wind that, if channeled carefully, could bring seeds, chairs and all things pleasant to us.

We are all would-be Presidents of the World, and kids kicking the sky that doesn't listen.

What would you do if you had only one penis and a one-way tube ticket and you wanted to fuck the whole nation in one come?

I know a professor of philosophy whose hobby is to quietly crush biscuit boxes in a supermarket.

Maybe you can send signed, plastic lighters to people in place of your penis. But then some people might take your lighter as a piece of sculpture and keep it on their living-room shelves.

So we go on eating and feeding frustration every day, lick lollipops and stay being peeping-toms dreaming of becoming Jack-The-Ripper.

This film was shot by our cameraman, Nick, while we were in a hospital. Nick is a gentleman, who prefers eating clouds and floating pies to shooting *Rape*. Nevertheless it was shot.

And as John says: "A is for parrot, which we can plainly see."

y.o. London, April 1969

Film still from *Rape*, 1969. Directed in collaboration with John Lennon.

Rape, a powerful and moving cinematic experience, is the closest of Ono's work to a narrative film. Yet like all her films it relies on a conceptual idea to determine the parameters of the action. The actual film appeared both staged and real, and this ambiguity gave it the added tension of authenticity.

As the title states, *Rape* is an examination of the invasion or violation of one person by another. The gripping narrative became a metaphor for life in the public eye, which had become part of Ono's life following her association with Lennon.

Cameraman Nic Knowland, Eva Majlath, and soundman Christian Wangler in a production photograph from the film *Rape*, 1969. Directed in collaboration with John Lennon.

Woman is the Nigger of the World

Woman is the nigger of the world
Yes she is ... think about it
Woman is the nigger of the world
Think about it ... do something about it.

We make her paint her face and dance
If she won't be a slave, we say that she don't love us
If she's real, we say she's trying to be a man
While putting her down we pretend that she's above us
Woman is the nigger of the world ... yes she is
If you don't believe me, take a look at the one you're with
Woman is the slave of the slaves
Ah, yeh ... better scream about it.

We make her bear and raise our children
And then we leave her flat for being a fat old mother hen
We tell her home is the only place she should be
Then we complain that she's too unworldly to be our friend
Woman is the nigger of the world ... yes she is
If you don't believe me, take a look at the one you're with
Woman is the slave to the slaves
Yeh (think about it).

We insult her everyday on TV
And wonder why she has no guts or confidence
When she's young we kill her will to be free
While telling her not to be so smart we put her down for being so dumb
Woman is the nigger of the world
Yes she is ... if you don't believe me, take a look at the one you're with
Woman is the slave to the slaves
Yes she is ... if you believe me, you better scream about it.

Repeat:
We make her paint her face and dance.
We make her paint her face and dance.
We make her paint her face and dance.

Ono and Lennon, 1972; song included in *Some Time in New York City*

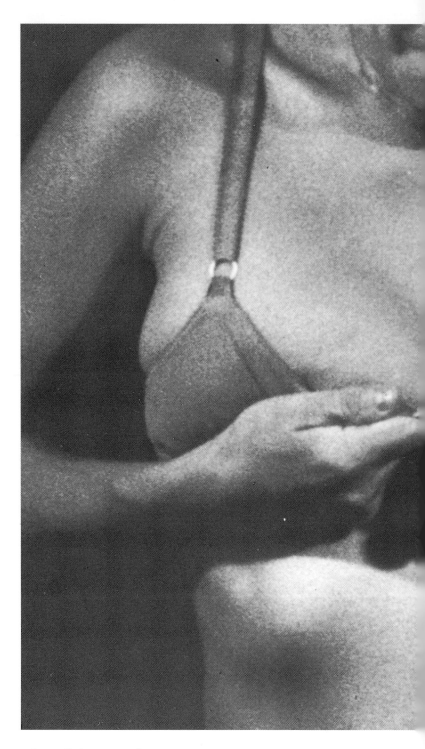

Film still from *Freedom,* 1970

In *Freedom* the camera focused on a woman (Yoko Ono) pulling at the clasp of her bra; the film ends just before it is removed. Here Ono played with our sense of anticipation and constructs a metaphor for the liberation of the female body and self.

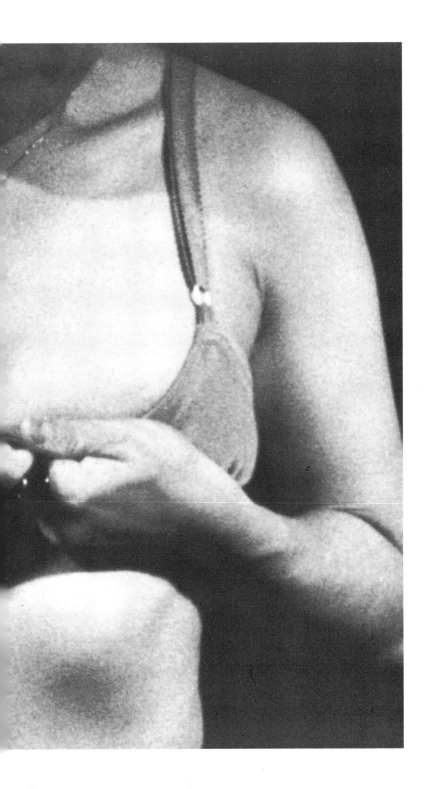

Sisters, O Sisters

We lost our green land
We lost our clean air
We lost our true wisdom
And we live in despair.

Sisters, O Sisters
Let's stand up right now
It's never too late
To start from the start.

Wisdom, O Wisdom
That's what we ask for
And yes, my dear sisters
We must learn to ask.

Middle 8:
Wisdom, O Wisdom
That's what we ask for
That's what we live for now.

Sisters, O Sisters
Let's wake up right on
It's never too late
To shout from our hearts.

Freedom, O Freedom
That's what we fight for
And yes, my dear sisters
We must learn to fight.

Middle 8:
Freedom, O Freedom
That's what we ask for
That's what we live for now.

Sisters, O Sisters
Let's give up no more
It's never too late
To build a new world.

New world, O New world
That's what we live for
And yes, my dear sisters
We must learn to live.

Middle 8:
New world, O New world
That's what we live for
That's what we must learn to build.

New world, O New world
That's what we live for
That's what we must learn to build.

y.o. 1972; song included in *Some Time in New York City*

BODY INNOCENCE

Allied to Ono's gender consciousness is her assault on the conventions of sexual morality. For her, sex and the human body are natural parts of life; to shun them is to deny a vital part of life. Typically, Ono eschewed a didactic response to these issues in her work. She elicited new ways of thinking about what constitutes pornography by presenting everyday scenes and neutral images under the banner of sexual freedom.

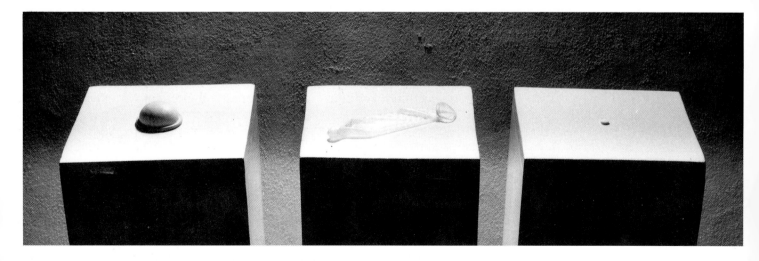

Object in Three Parts, 1966

Object in Three Parts, with its diaphragm, condom, and birth control pill, blatantly challenges the hypocritical morality that calls for silence on all matters sexual. Its willingness to openly address these issues mirrors Ono's acceptance of body functions and body parts as natural.

Tony Cox, unidentified performer, and Ono during the London production of *No. 4 (Bottoms)*, 1966

No. 4 (Bottoms) is the film with which Ono is most identified. Its implicit challenge to England's strict censorship laws led to an injunction—later overturned—against releasing the film commercially. The conceptual design of the film—recording moving images of people's backsides—established a framework in which a repetitive action takes place. Compositionally, the centered buttocks created a quasi-abstract, four-part division of space—a four-way conversation as Ono termed it. Cinematically, Ono's selection of a moving image and her elimination of all background space caused the screen itself to seem to be moving. Within the framework of its straightforward and literal cinematography and repetitive action, the imagery is full of variety. Though apparently simple, *No. 4 (Bottoms)* addresses larger issues of difference and expressiveness within the body politic.

Initially, the film was silent; its rhythm was to be the "very basic, simple beat" of the moving bottoms. But the contrast between the simplicity of the image and the complexity of the dialogue that occurred during the shooting of the film encouraged Ono to use these conversations as the soundtrack in the second version. Thus, as with many of her performances, the sound component was not artificial but emerged directly from the process of executing the work. For Ono, the pseudo-intellectuality of the conversations set up an interesting tension with the purity of the image. "The image is so pure ... we have incredibly innocent, beautiful bodies. The movement they create is so simple and beautiful—beautiful because it is so simple. And then there is all this chattering going on in our minds."

On Film No. 4
(in taking the bottoms of 365 saints of our time)

I wonder why men can get serious at all. They have this delicate long thing hanging outside their bodies, which goes up and down by its own will. First of all having it outside your body is terribly dangerous. If I were a man I would have a fantastic castration complex to the point that I wouldn't be able to do a thing. Second, the inconsistency of it, like carrying a chance time alarm or something. If I were a man I would always be laughing at myself. Humour is probably something the male of the species discovered through their own anatomy. But men are so serious. Why? Why violence? Why hatred? Why war? If people want to make war, they should make a colour war, and paint each others city up during the night in pinks and greens. Men have an unusual talent for making a bore out of everything they touch. Art, painting, sculpture, like who wants a cast-iron woman, for instance.

The film world is becoming terribly aristocratic, too. It's professionalism all the way down the line. In any other field: painting, music, etc., people are starting to become iconoclastic. But in the film world—that's where nobody touches it except the director. The director carries the old mystery of the artist. He is creating a universe, a mood, he is unique, etc., etc. This film proves that anybody can be a director. A film-maker in San Francisco wrote to me and asked if he could make the San Francisco version of *No. 4*. That's OK with me. Somebody else wrote from New York [that] she wants to make a slow-motion version with her own behind. That's OK, too. I'm hoping that after seeing this film people will start to make their own home movies like crazy.

In 50 years or so, which is like 10 centuries from now, people will look at the films of the 60's. They will probably comment on Ingmar Bergman as meaningfully meaningful film-maker, Jean Luc Godard as the meaningfully meaningless, Antonioni as meaninglessly meaningful, etc., etc. Then they would come to the *No. 4* film and see a sudden swarm of exposed bottoms, that these bottoms, in fact, belonged to people who represented the London scene. And I hope that they would see that the 60's was not only the age of achievements, but of laughter. This film, in fact, is like an aimless petition signed by people with their anuses. Next time we wish to make an appeal, we should send this film as the signature list.

My ultimate goal in film-making is to make a film which includes a smiling face snap of every single human being in the world. Of course, I cannot go around the whole world and take the shots myself. I need cooperation from something like the post offices of the world. If everybody would drop a snapshot of themselves and their families to the post office of their town, or allow themselves to be photographed by the nearest photographic studio, this would be soon accomplished.

Of course, this film would need constant adding of footage. Probably nobody would like to see the whole film at once, so you can keep it in a library or something, and when you want to see some particular town's people's smiling faces you can go and check that section of film. We can also arrange it with a television network so that whenever you want to see faces of a particular location in the world, all you have to do is to press a button and there it is. This way, if Johnson wants to see what sort of people he killed in Vietnam that day, he only has to turn the channel. Before this you were just part of a figure in the newspapers, but after this you become a smiling face. And when you are born, you will know that if you wanted to, you will have in your life time to communicate with the whole world. That is more than most of us could ask for. Very soon, the age may come where we would not need photographs to communicate, like ESP, etc. It will happen soon, but that will be "After the Film Age."

y.o. 1967

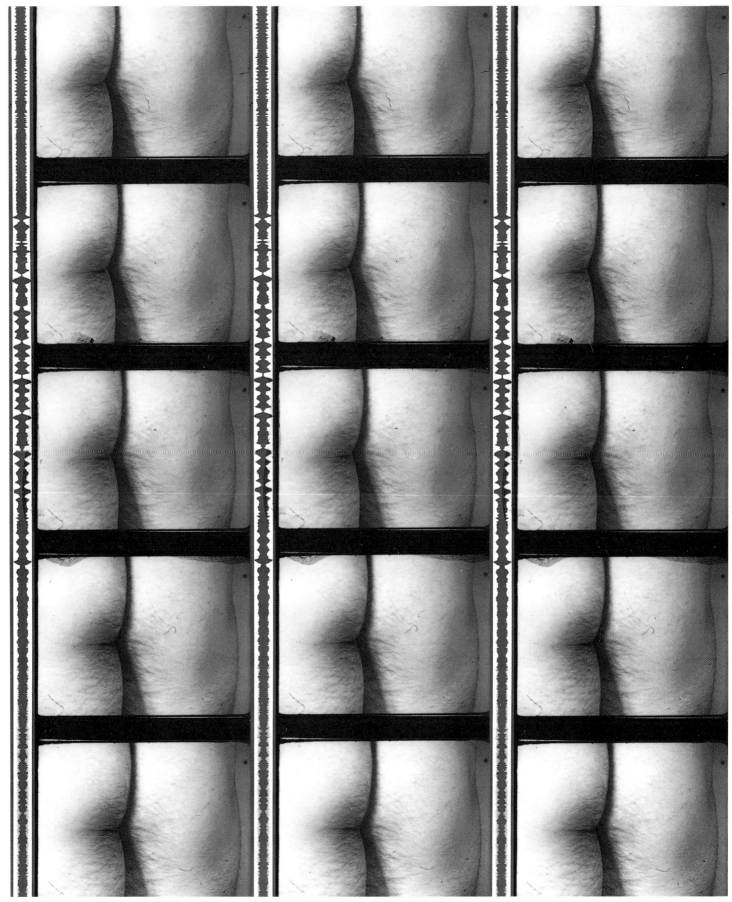
Filmstrip from *No. 4 (Bottoms)*, 1966

Film No. 6
A Contemporary Sexual Manual
(366 sexual positions)
(unrealized film script)

1-1/2 hour color separate soundtrack. Cast: a woman, a man, and a child.

The whole film takes place in a bedroom with a large double bed in the center and a window at the foot of the bed.

The film is a family scene of a quiet couple and a four year old daughter lying on the bed for the whole night. All they do is just sleep, and the 366 sexual positions are all in the mind of the audience. But this is not Andy Warhol: in a sense this is basically a clean, healthy heterosexual scene spared from boredom.

The delicate change of positions made by the threesome has a slow erotic dance movement quality to it on one hand, and a comfortable domestic nature (scratching each other, etc.) on the other.

The contemporary sex, unlike what you see in blue films, reflects the complexity of our society, and it is subtle and multi-leveled. So in this film, you never see an obvious position as two people on top of each other, or actually making love in any form. They very rarely exchange words with each other and when they do, the sound is not synchronized so all you see is their mouth[s] moving. But there is definitely an air of peaceful unity and coziness among the three.

The whole thing would be done in a way so that it would definitely pass the censors: which is a commercially important factor. There is no need to show the genitals, etc., though we're not going to do one of those "under the sheets" scene, either.

There are occasional breaks that take place in the film: going to the toilet, for instance, (in which case, all you see is one of them getting up and going out of the room and coming back).

The camera will start panning from under the bed, then the foot of the bed, gradually going up, and finally up over their heads until the window at the foot of the bed starts to cover the whole screen. This camera movement can be compared to the moon rising and then disappearing at the other end in the time space of 1-1/2 hours.

The soundtrack in contrast to the screen consists mainly of tragic conversations between a couple who are about to split, whimpering of a child, whispers, sighs, and love groans. Also, a sound-tape from a Trafalgar square soap-bubble happening comes in as if they are sounds in a dream of one of them, or of the three, while they sleep. At dawn, milk bottle rattling and bird sounds will come in, and the film will end with increasingly heavy bird sound.

y.o. 1968

Censored front cover of Lennon and Ono's album *Two Virgins,* 1968

Ono and Lennon's album *Two Virgins* was censored because of the frontal and posterior nudity that graced the album's front and back covers. Censors demanded that sleeves be placed over the album so that only the faces of Ono and Lennon would be visible.

Film No. 12
(Up Your Legs Forever)

The camera work of the film should constantly go up, up, up, non-stop. Collect 367 pairs of legs and, just go up the legs (from toes to the end of thighs) pair after pair and go on up until you run through the whole 367.

y.o. 1967

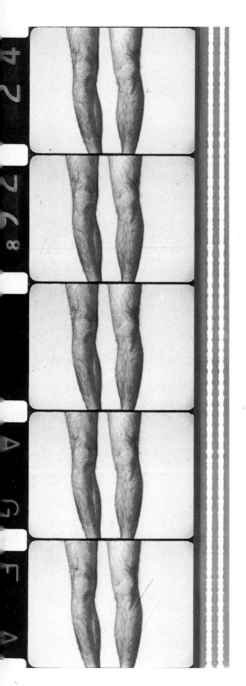

Filmstrip from *Up Your Legs Forever*, 1970

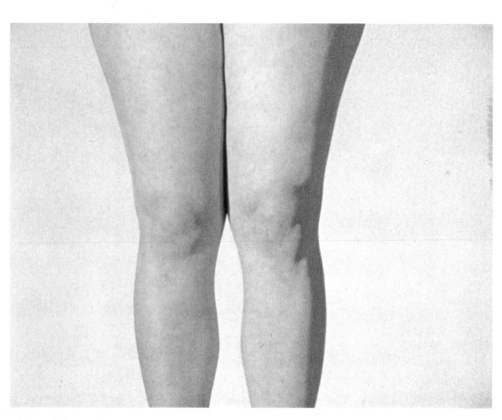

Film still from *Up Your Legs Forever*, 1970

Up Your Legs Forever, like *Bottoms,* focuses on a particular part of the anatomy—in this case legs. Once again, Ono created a production process which allowed the film to develop like a musical score: variation within a repetitive theme. Far from being threatening, *Up Your Legs Forever* is a witty celebration of the body as paradigmatic subject matter.

Imaginary Film Series
Shi (From the cradle to the grave of Mr. So)

A slow film taken in the time space of 60 years, following a person who's born and died. From about the 30th year, it becomes a film of a couple, as the man gets married. It really becomes "a film of waiting" towards the end since the film obviously starts to have a senile quality in its camera work, while the man in the film looks still robust. It is amazing that the death came so suddenly over the man in a form of diarrhea. Highly incredible film which makes one think.—You never know when you die.

y.o.

Filmstrip from *Erection*, 1971. Produced and directed in collaboration with John Lennon.

In *Erection*, Ono and Lennon playfully deny our expectation of sexual display by recording the construction of a building.

POLITICAL ACTIVISM

War Is Over billboard in Times Square, New York, 1969

Ono believed that the "job of the artist is not to destroy but to change the value of things." For her, this entailed bringing about a world where there was universal freedom and peace. Following her conviction that the mind is omnipresent, she held that change could be materialized through wishing—specifically, through the affirmative wishing associated with love.

Acting on this theory, Ono and John Lennon initiated and participated in a great many art events related to peace. Some, like *Bed-In* and *War is Over*, drew on Ono's view of the efficacy of positive wishing. Others, such as their participation in the charity pop concert on behalf of the United Nations Children's Fund at the Lyceum Ballroom in London, constituted more practical efforts at fund-raising.

War Is Over billboard on Corso Rinascimento, Rome, Italy, 1969

The affirmation that "War Is Over," which appeared on billboards in cities around the world in 1969, manifested Ono's conviction that wishing could effect transformation.

If people make it a habit to draw a somersault on every other street as they commute to their office, take off their pants before they fight, shake hands with strangers whenever they feel like, give flowers or part of their clothing on streets, subways, elevator[s], toilet[s], etc., and if politicians go through a tea house door (lowered, so people must bend very low to get through) before they discuss anything and spend a day watching the fountain water dance at the nearest park, the world business may slow down a little but we may have peace.

To me this is dance.

From Ono's *To the Wesleyan People*, 1966

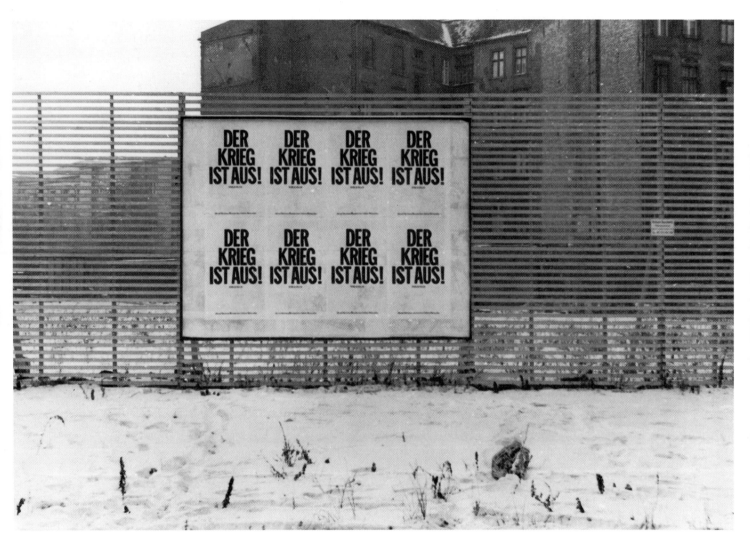

War Is Over posters in Berlin, Germany, 1969

What Is the Relationship Between the World and the Artist?

Many people believe that in this age, art is dead. They despise the artists who show in galleries and are caught up in the traditional art world. Artists themselves are beginning to lose their confidence. They don't know whether they are doing something that still has value in this day and age where the social problems are so vital and critical. I wondered myself about this. Why am I still an artist? And why am I not joining the violent revolutionaries? Then I realized that destruction is not my game. Violent revolutionaries are trying to destroy the establishment. That is good. But how? By killing? Killing is such an artless thing. All you need is a Coke bottle in your hand and you can kill. But people who kill that way most often become the next establishment after they've killed the old. Because they are using the same method that the old establishment used to destroy. Violent revolutionaries' thinking is very close to establishment-type thinking and ways of solving problems.

I like to fight the establishment by using methods that are so far removed from establishment-type thinking that the establishment doesn't know how to fight back. For instance, they cannot stamp out John and Yoko events *Two Virgins, Bed Peace, Acorn Peace*, and *War Is Over* poster event.

Artists are not here to destroy or to create. *Creating* is just as simple and artless a thing to do as *destroying*. Everyone on earth has creativity. Even a housewife can create a baby. Children are just as creative as the people whom society considers artists. Creative artists are just good enough to be considered children. Artists must not create more objects, the world is full of everything it needs. I'm bored with artists who make big lumps of sculpture and occupy a big space with them and think they have done something *creative* and allow people nothing but to applaud the lump. That is sheer narcissism. Why don't they at least let people touch them? Money and space are wasted on such projects when there are people starving and people who don't have enough space to sleep or breathe.

The job of an artist is not to destroy but to change the value of things. And by doing that, artists can change the world into a Utopia where there is total freedom for everybody. That can be achieved only when there is total communication in the world. Total communication equals peace. That is our aim. That is what artists can do for the world!

In order to change the value of things, you've got to know about life and the situation of the world. You have to be more than a child.

That is the difference between a child's work and an artist's work. That is the difference between an artist's work and a murderer's work. We are artists. Artist is just a frame of mind. Anybody can be an artist. It doesn't involve having a talent. It involves only having a certain frame of mind, an attitude, determination, and imagination that springs naturally out of the necessity of the situation.

Examples of today's living artists:

There was a temple in Japan called the Golden Temple. A man loved it very much as it was, and he couldn't stand the thought of anything happening to it. He felt the only way he could stop anything from happening to it was to burn it down, and he did. Now, the image of the temple was able to stay forever in his mind as a perfect form.

There was a man who made a counterfeit one thousand yen. It circulated with no trouble at all. The man travelled to another city and circulated another counterfeit one thousand yen. If he made lots of counterfeit money he could have been discovered right away. But he wasn't interested in making lots of money. He wanted to have fun and play a subtle game. The police went wild and announced that if anybody found a counterfeit one thousand yen they would get two thousand yen as a reward if they came to the police station. This man changed the value of money by his actions.

In this very same sense, we have artists today whose works move beyond the gallery space and help change the world: Abby Hoffman, Jerry Rubin, Paul Krassner, for instance, and many others. They radiate something that is sensitive and artistic in a very renaissance sense, when the majority of so-called artists these days are hardcore businessmen. Message is the medium. There are only two classes left in our society. The class who communicates and the class who doesn't. Tomorrow I hope there will be just one. Total communication equals peace.

Men can destroy/Women can create/Artists revalue

Bed-In—also known as *Bed Peace*—as presented in inner gatefold of Lennon and Ono's *Wedding Album*, 1969

Bed-In was a peace demonstration that Ono and Lennon staged in a bedroom of an Amsterdam Hotel in 1969. "The message of peace was the strongest idea," Ono later said of *Bed-In*, "but there was also the message of love—men and women being able to make a statement together—and the West and East coming together."

The film *Bed-In*, produced in Montreal in June 1969, is a straightforward documentary. It is also a visual record of the late 1960s search for peace during the Vietnam War. In this film Ono and Lennon became the subjects, not within a conceptual or performance structure as in their other films, but as activists using their celebrity as a means to bring attention to issues that concerned them. Here the public persona was not critiqued or hidden from view but was used as a means to an end—the search for a positive, constructive, and poetic search for peace.

Now or Never

Are we gonna keep pushing our children to drugs
Are we gonna keep driving them insane
Are we gonna keep laying empty words and fists
Are we gonna be remembered as the century that failed

People of America
When will we learn
It's now or never
There's no time to lose

Are we gonna keep sending our youth to war
Are we gonna keep scarring ricefields and infants
Are we gonna keep watching dead bodies over dinner
Are we gonna be known as the century that kills

People of America
When will we stop
It's now or never
There's no time to waste

Are we gonna keep pretending things are alright
Are we gonna keep our mouth closed just in case
Are we gonna keep putting off until it's too late
Are we gonna be known as the century of fear

People of America when will we see
It's now or never
We've no time to lose

Are we gonna keep digging oil wells and gold
Are we gonna keep shooting the ones that try to change
Are we gonna keep thinking it won't happen to us
Are we gonna be known as the century that kills

People of America
Please listen to your soul
We can change the times
To century of hope

Cause

Dream you dream alone is only a dream
But dream we dream together is reality

y.o. 1972; song included in *Approximately Infinite Universe*

Angela

Angela, they put you in prison
Angela, they shot down your man
Angela, you're one of the millions of political
    prisoners in the world.

Sister, there's a wind that never dies
Sister, we're breathing together
Sister, our love and hopes forever keep on
    moving oh so slowly in the world.

Angela, can you hear the earth is turning?
Angela, the world watches you.
Angela, you soon will be returning to your
    sisters and brothers of the world.

Sister, you're still a people teacher
Sister, your word reaches far
Sister, there's a million different races but
    we all share the same future in the
    world.

Chorus:
They gave you sunshine
They gave you sea
They gave you everything but the jailhouse
    key.
They gave you coffee
They gave you tea
They gave you everything but equality.

Ono and Lennon, 1972;
song included in *Some Time in New York City*

I See Rainbows

It's getting cold around here
People living in fear
Whether it's a country or an island
Frighten[ed] of death
Holding our breath
While our souls cry out

I don't wanna be mugged by some mother
I don't wanna be shot for ten dollar[s]
What's this talk about limited holocaust
Have a heart, I don't even want my roof to
    leak

I see rainbows
I see tomorrow
I see us sending rainbow love
I see rainbows
I see tomorrow
I see us sending rainbow thoughts

I don't wanna be part of terrorists
I don't wanna be one of survivalists
This is our world and it's beautiful
I wanna survive survive survive together

I see rainbows
I see tomorrow
I see us sending rainbow love
I see rainbow[s]
I see tomorrow
I see us sending rainbow thoughts

y.o. 1982; song included in *It's Alright*

In the summer of '72 in New York City, John and I invited the press to announce the founding of a conceptual country called Nutopia. Anybody could be a citizen of this country. Citizens were automatically the country's ambassadors. The country's body was the airfield of our joint thoughts. Its constitution was our love, and its spirit, our dreams. Its flag was the white flag of surrender. A surrender to peace. We wished that one day we would take the flag to the United Nations and place it alongside the other flags as Nutopia was just another concept, as were concepts such as France, United States, and the Soviet Union. It was not a concept founded to threaten any other. At the time, the idea of "surrender" did not go down too well. A radical friend of ours expressed that he, too, disliked the term. "Surrender sounds like defeat," he said. "Well, don't you surrender to love, for instance?" I looked at him. "No, he wouldn't," I thought. "Are women the only people who know the pride and joy of surrender?" I wondered. "It's a waste of time to explain to a macho radical, didn't I tell you?" said John, a man who surrendered to the world, life, and finally to Universe. "Anyway, don't worry, Yoko. One day we'll put it up there. You and I. I promise." I still believe we will.

It is time for you to rise. It is you who will raise the flag. I feel that John and I, as a unit, have done our share. The rest of my life belongs to our son, Sean. It is your effort. Your flag. So remember, We Are Family. You and I are Unity. In the Joy of Harmony, the World is One to Infinity. Speak out. Speak out of love and you need not fear. We will hear. America The Beautiful. Surrender to Peace. I love you. Yoko Ono Lennon, December 25 '82, New York City.

Excerpt from *Surrender to Peace*; printed in *The New York Times*, January 24, 1983

Dedication inscribed on the cover of Ono's album *Feeling the Space*, 1973

This album is dedicated to the sisters
who died in pain and sorrow
and those who are now
in prisons and in mental hospitals
for being unable to survive
in the male society.

EVOCATIONS OF

From front cover of Lennon and Ono's boxed album set, *Wedding Album*, 1969

Dreamy evocations of romantic interconnectedness entered Ono's work after 1968. Gone were the paradox and self-conscious challenge to orthodox aesthetic conventions that had characterized her earlier endeavors. In their place were intimate recordings of tender moments between herself and John Lennon and poetic visualizations of the fusion of their beings. Appropriately, these evocations of love were expressed in media which possess an inherent narrative—films, photographic album covers, and lyrics.

LOVE

Every Man Has a Woman Who Loves Him

Every man has a woman who loves him
In rain or shine or life or death
If he finds her in this life time
He will know when he presses his ear to
    her breast

Why do I roam when I know you're the one
Why do I laugh when I feel like crying

Every woman has a man who loves her
Rise or fall of her life and in death
If she finds him in this life time
She will know when she looks into his eyes

Why do I roam when I know you're the one
Why do I run when I feel like holding you

Every man has a woman who loves him
If he finds her in this life time
He will know

    y.o. 1980; song included in Double Fantasy

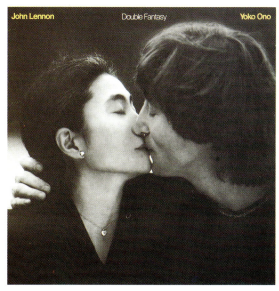

Front cover of Lennon and Ono's album *Double Fantasy*, 1980

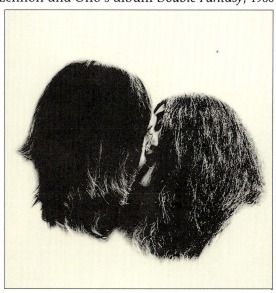

Front album cover of Lennon and Ono's *Wedding Album*, 1969

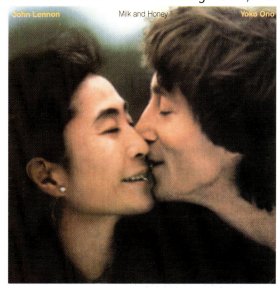

Front cover of Lennon and Ono's album *Milk and Honey*, 1984

On *Film No. 5* (known as *Smile*) and *Two Virgins*

Last year, I said I'd like to make a "smile film" which included a smiling face snap of every single human being in the world. But that had obvious technical difficulties and it was very likely that the plan would have remained as one of my beautiful never-nevers.

This year, I started off thinking of making films that were meant to be shown in a 100 years' time: i.e. taking different city views, hoping that most of the buildings in them would be demolished by the time the film was released; shooting an ordinary woman with her full gear—knowing that in a 100 years' time, she'd look extraordinary, etc., etc. It's to apply the process of making vintage wine to film-making. This, in practice, would mean that as a film-maker you don't really have to make a film anymore but just put your name (that is, if you so wish) on any film and store it. Storing would then become the main endeavor of a film-maker. But then, the idea started to get too conceptual. That's the trouble with all my strawberries. They tend to evaporate and I find myself lying on the floor doing nothing.

One afternoon, John and I went out in the garden and shot *Film No. 5,* the smile film, and *Two Virgins.* They were done in a spirit of home movies. In both films, we were mainly concerned about the vibrations the films send out—the kind that was between us. But, with *Film No. 5,* a lot of planning, working, and talking out things had preceded the afternoon. For instance, I had thought of making *Film No. 5* into a *Dr. Zhivago* and let it go on for 4 hours with an intermission and all that, but later decided to stick to a more commercial length of an hour (approx.). 8 mm. copies of the film are also available for people who'd like to have the film on their wall as a light-portrait. Also, we'll store some copies for the next century.

They say that in the corner of the world there is a man who sits and spends his life in sending good vibrations to the world, and when a star twinkles, we are only catching the twinkle that was sent 1,000 light years ago, etc.

Imagine a painting that smiles just once in a billion years. John's ghostly smile in *Film No. 5* might just communicate in a hundred years' time, or maybe, the way things are rolling, it may communicate much earlier than that. I think all the doors are just ready to open now. One light knock should do. It's just that there are still a minority group in the world who are afraid of the doorless world to come. They're just not sure how they can cope with it. But most of us know that doors are just figments of our imagination. The good thing is, though, that law of nature that once you know, you can never unknow things, so the doors are going to disappear pretty rapidly, I think.

Some critic recently commented on us, John and I, as being lollypop artists who are preoccupied with blowing soap-bubbles forever. I thought that was beautiful. There's a lot you can do with blowing soap-bubbles. Maybe the future USA should decide their presidency by having a soap-bubble contest. Blowing soap-bubbles could be used as a form of swearing. Some day the whole world can make it its occupation to blow soap-bubbles.

Would they ever know that Johnny West and Yoko DeMille ate bananas together?

y.o. October 22, 1968

Mona Lisa & Her Smile
(unrealized film script)

Ask audience to stare at a figure (any figure) for a long time and then immediately turn their eyes to the screen and see the reflection.

y.o.

Film still from *Film No. 5 (Smile)*, 1968

In *Film No. 5 (Smile)*, Ono used the capacity of film to alter time to create a unique visual portrait. The film consisted of a single shot of John Lennon, in soft focus, standing in a garden. The 3 minutes of film were then printed with multiple frames to create a running time of 52 minutes. The film recorded subtle and evocative changes in John's facial expression and magnified his gestures and emotions.

Film No. 9
Don't Worry Love
(unrealized film script)

1/2 hour to 45 minutes. Colour highspeed camera; synchronized sound.

This is a love message we send from England to all over the world and to the future.

The idea was conceived from the fact that when a star blinks, we only perceive it 2000 years after it's actually blinked. And they say that the love we feel now is the love that's been conceived by somebody 2000 years ago, or that somebody in the corner of the world is sending love vibrations just to keep us in love, etc.

The film will be 20 seconds each shot of people smiling and saying "don't worry love," but because the shots are done in highspeed, each smile would actually be synchronized to the highspeed motion so that what you actually hear would be a strange elongated version of "don't worry love."

I hope this film will make the whole world a shade happier and rosier, and that our smile would encourage people of 2000 years later, just as the blinking of stars. It is actually a film that would be most effective if it's seen in our great, great grandchildren's time.

We must get a galaxy of people with strong good vibrations to smile in this film—people who represent our age.

y.o. 1968

Film still from *Two Virgins*, 1968

The film *Two Virgins* (1968), produced in collaboration with Lennon, celebrated their relationship through the filmic superimposition of their faces over each other. As the film plays through its 19-minute running time, the viewer explores the two faces as they play off each other. The colors, shadows, light, and movement of their expressions compose a softly lyrical, dual self-portrait. *Two Virgins* expressed Ono and Lennon's idea of themselves as a joined persona through which they shared their creative energies.

Film still from *Imagine*, 1971. In collaboration with John Lennon.

Imagine is the best-known film collaboration of Ono and Lennon. Begun as an accompaniment to the recording *Imagine*, this 70-minute film illustrated the soundtrack with found images and improvised scenes of Ono and Lennon's life. It is an optimistic, celebratory film—a musical adventure of friendship, love, and fellowship. Structurally, *Imagine* anticipated the music video phenomenon which emerged in the 1980s. It highlighted, rather than worked against, film as a recording of life.

Back cover of exhibition brochure *This Is Not Here*, Everson Museum of Art, Syracuse, New York, 1971.

Ono's retrospective at the Everson Museum, Syracuse, New York, in 1971, featured John Lennon as guest artist. As an affirmation of what they viewed as their fused beings, they superimposed images of their faces on the back cover of the exhibition catalogue—an echo of *Two Virgins* and a presage of the later merger of their names into the trademark Lenono.

Approximately Infinite Universe

John and I were having a conversation about astral identity. John was in a mood to start it off with a "No" and I with a "Yes." It's a seesaw game we play—though we prefer to think of it as a dialectic thinking process we developed between us, and that the seesaw will grow a propeller and start to float in the air, if we seesawed enough. So! We were ruminating on astral identity.

It's a bit uhh, you know.

Right, But you know how an arbitrary number-series starts to make a pattern and repeats itself in the end. Say if the universe is infinite sometime or other it may start to repeat itself.

Still, the idea of John from Liverpool and Yoko from Tokyo existing on another planet as well, having tea when we were having tea, that sort of thing, was a bit too much, John said, and his beautiful toes started to move up and down in bed.

Maybe there's a timewarp and they'd be doing something we did last year, John. You're just offended. Men feel threatened when their uniqueness is questioned.

Not that. It just means that you believe in fatalism.

Not necessarily. It only means that there are many, many universes. Infinite numbers of.

Infinity is just a man-made concept, it doesn't exist.

Look, take numbers. Numbers are a concept, too. There's no such thing as number one, say. It's actually a number that is an infinite approximation to number one, that we call number one. Like 0.999999 ... to infinity but we build bridges and buildings on those infinitely approximate numbers not on definite ones. That means that we are always just on the verge of things, verge of being. That goes for buildings and ships and everything.

John turned into an English teapot before my eyes, and I found myself drifting off to a cosmic nowhere by myself.

If it works on a microcosmic world like numbers below one, why not out there in the universe? Universe is infinitely approximate. But that means that it's at least approximately infinite, right? So, the concept of infinity is not just a romanticism, John. It *is* an approximately infinite universe.

I heard a tiny grunt and John saying he liked the sound of the words. Then suddenly we realized that this time we were both drifting out in a cosmos somewhere together, like God's two little dandruffs floating in the universe.

"Astral identity! Wow!" "Something else, right?" "Right!"

Later, we came down to Earth and went back to our weekly ceremony of washing our hair and helping each other dry it.

Liner notes from Ono's album *Approximately Infinite Universe*, 1973

Poster included in Ono's album *Fly*, 1971

VANGUARD VOCALS

Program cover from Ornette Coleman's Royal Albert Hall concert, London, February 29, 1968.

When Ono turned her attention to popular music and film, she did not abandon her vanguard roots; she simply brought them into new realms. Her music contained the same kind of aural material that had characterized her earlier performance works such as *Toilet Piece* and *A Grapefruit in the World of Park*, with its high-pitched wails, moans, and a tape recording of words spoken backwards. At other times, Ono fused the worlds of popular music and vanguard art by using earlier performance texts or expository writing as lyrics—as in "Air Talk," whose lyrics first appeared as notes to her Lisson Gallery exhibition in 1967.

A striking example of Ono's early voice modulation work was her contribution to Ornette Coleman's concert at the Royal Albert Hall, London in 1968. As with her earlier vocal manipulations, this work exulted in the sound effects that would characterize Ono's later pop music. Her instructions to Coleman and his musicians were as follows:

To Ornette

Do not be concerned about showing many things: simplicity and economy of notes, dynamics and rhythm.
Think of the days when you only had one heart and one penis to give—and one note.
Think of the days when you had to suffer in silence for 10 days of eternity before you could give, and yet you were afraid of giving because what you were giving was so true and so total, you knew that you would suffer a death after that.
Think of the days when you allowed silences in your life for dreaming and thinking of dreaming.
This is no shit. No "mood" or whatever you call it. It's real.
Four of you play like four cats used to chattering with each other. Forget about each other.
Forget about what you've learnt or heard in the music academy world or the like. Be insecure.
    (You should bind one hand and play with one hand if that makes you insecure, or blindfold for this piece.)

<u>Section one:</u>
I will call.
don't respond until you are really ready.
respond with same plaintiveness—of one note and slight variation.
Or you should call to seek for other voices.
<u>Section two:</u>
total silence—let's see how long we can hold it, or how long it is necessary.
it is the most tenderest of silences—of making love.
<u>Section three:</u>
let's gradually go up—don't go up too quickly. Listen to me. I will try to control you from going up, awkward breaks that are caused by that are part of the music.
and when we are up, stay there until we are completely exhausted—and really, so that the section four will be no fake.
<u>Section four:</u>
very quiet, your exhausted self.
just breathe with your instrument
die down.

y.o. 1968

Air Talk

It's sad that the air is the only
    thing we share.
No matter how close we get to each other,
    there is always air between us.

It's also nice that we share the air.
No matter how far apart we are,
    the air links us.

y.o., *Yoko Ono at Lisson*, Lisson Gallery, London, 1967;
expanded for *Approximately Infinite Universe*, 1973

Sunday Bloody Sunday

Well it was Sunday bloody Sunday
When they shot the people there
The crys of thirteen martyrs
Filled the Free Derry air.
Is there any one amongst you
Dare to blame it on the kids?
Not a soldier boy was bleeding
When they nailed the coffin lids!

Sunday bloody Sunday
Bloody Sunday's the day!

You claim to be majority
Well you know that it's a lie
You're really a minority
On this sweet emerald isle.
When Stormont bans our marches
They've got a lot to learn
Internment is no answer
It's those mothers' turn to burn!

Sunday bloody Sunday
Bloody Sunday's the day!

You anglo pigs and scotties
Sent to colonize the North
You wave your bloody Union Jacks
And you know what it's worth!
How dare you hold to ransom
A people proud and free
Keep Ireland for the Irish
Put the English back to sea!

Sunday bloody Sunday
Bloody Sunday's the day!

Yes it's always bloody Sunday
In the concentration camps
Keep Falls Road free forever
From the bloody English hands
Repatriate to Britain
All of you who call it home
Leave Ireland to the Irish
Not for London or for Rome!

Sunday bloody Sunday
Bloody Sunday's the day!

Song by Ono and Lennon; included in *Some Time in New York City*, 1972

Kiss Kiss Kiss

Kiss kiss kiss kiss me love
Just one kiss, kiss will do
Kiss kiss kiss kiss me love
Just one kiss, kiss will do

Why death
Why life
Warm hearts
Cold darts

Kiss kiss kiss kiss me love
I'm bleeding inside

It's a long, long story to tell
And I can only show you my hell

Touch touch touch touch me love
Just one touch, touch will do
Touch touch touch touch me love
Just one touch, touch will do

Why me
Why you
Broken mirror
White terror

Touch touch touch touch me love
I'm shaking inside

It's that faint faint sound of the childhood bell
Ringing inside my soul

Kiss kiss kiss kiss me love
Just one kiss, kiss will do

y.o. 1980; song included in *Double Fantasy*

Front cover of Yoko Ono and John Lennon's album
Unfinished Music No. 2: Life with the Lions, 1967

Front cover of the album *Yoko Ono/Plastic Ono Band*, 1970

No, No, No

Let me take my scarf off
No, no, no
Don't help me I can do it
And you know it
Don't touch me I don't like it

Let me take my blouse off
No, no, no
Don't help me I can do it
And you know it
Don't touch me I don't like it

You promised me
You promised me
You promised me
You promised me
I don't remember what you promised
I know you didn't keep it

Let me take my pants off
No, no, no
Don't hold me, I don't want it
You're thinking Rock Hudson when we do it

Let me take my ring off
No, no, no
Don't do it, I can't do it
I'm seeing broken glass when we do it

You promised me
You promised me
You promised me
You promised me
I don't remember what we promised
But I know we didn't keep it

You promised me
You promised me
You promised me
You promised me
I don't remember what we promised
But I miss you!

y.o. 1981; song included in *Season of Glass*

Front cover of *Approximately Infinite Universe,* 1973

Front cover of *Feeling the Space,* 1973

Hell in Paradise

This is Hell in Paradise
We're all asleep or paralyzed
Why are we scared to verbalize
Our multicolor dreams

When will we come to realize
We're all stoned or passified [sic]
While the boogie men organize
Their multilevel schemes

Underqualified for love
Overqualified for life
Sticking our heads in slime
Thinking we're in our prime

Mesmerized by mythology
Hypnotized by ideology
Antagonized by reality
Vandalized by insanity
Desensitized by fraternity
Sanitized by policy
Jeopardized by lunacy

Penalized by apathy
And living in the world of fantasy
Dancing on hot coal
Waiting for the last call
It's Adam's ball
Eve's call

Wake up, shake up, check out, work out, speak out, reach out, it's time to, time to, time to, to, to, to, to . . . .

This is Hell in Paradise
None of us wish to recognize
But do we want them to materialize
An endangered species . . . .

Exorcize institution
Exercise intuition
Mobilize transition
With inspiration for life

y.o. 1985; song included in *Starpeace*

Front cover of *Starpeace,* 1985

MOURNING

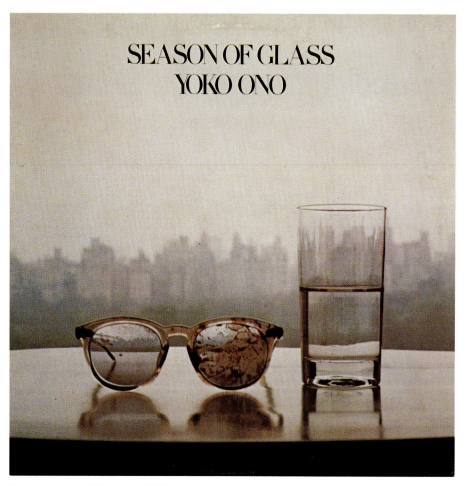

Front cover of *Season of Glass*, 1981

Strawberry Fields Forever

In Memory of John Lennon, New York City has designated a beautiful triangular island in Central Park to be known as Strawberry Fields. It happens to be where John and I took our last walk together. John would have been very proud that this was given to him, an island named after his song, rather than a statue or a monument.

My initial thought was to acquire some English and Japanese plants and give them to the park commission to be planted in Strawberry Fields. But somehow that idea was not quite in the spirit of things. Then I remembered what John and I did when we first met over ten years ago. We planted an acorn in England as a symbol of our love. We then sent acorns to all the heads of state around the world, inviting them to do the same. Many responded saying that they enjoyed the experience.

So in the name of John and Yoko, and spirit of love and sharing, I would like to once again invite all countries of the world, this time to offer plants, rocks, and/or stones of their nations for Strawberry Fields. The plants will eventually be forests, the rocks will be a resting place for traveling souls, the bricks will pave the lane John and I used to walk on and the circle where we used to sit and talk for hours. It will be nice to have the whole world in one place, one field, living and growing together in harmony. This will be the nicest tribute we could give to John. The acorn we planted a decade ago is now a tree. I would like to obtain a twig from it to be transplanted on the island. Maybe we could add a moonstone or a pebble from Mars, so as not to shut out the universe.
The invitation is open!

Copies of this note will be sent to Mayor Koch, who has been a major inspiration behind the designation of Strawberry Fields, and to heads of state throughout the world. Let me take you to Strawberry Fields.

y.o. 1981

Video still from *Walking on Thin Ice*, 1981

The song "Walking on Thin Ice" was written in 1980 prior to Lennon's murder. The following year, Ono released it as a single and created an accompanying music video whose footage of Ono and Lennon together memorialized their relationship.

Walking on Thin Ice

Walking on thin ice
I'm paying the price
For throwing the dice in the air
Why must we learn it the hard way
And play the game of life with your heart

I gave you my knife
You gave me my life
Like a gush of wind in my hair
Why do we forget what's been said
And play the game of life with our hearts

I may cry some day
But the tears will dry whichever way
And when our hearts return to ashes
It'll be just a story
It'll be just a story

ice ice ice ice ice ice ice ice ice ice ice ice
ice ice ice ice ice ice ice ice ice ice ice ice
ice ice ice ice ice ice ice ice ice ice ice ice
ice ice ice ice ice ice ice ice ice ice ice ice
ice ice ice ice ice ice ice ice ice ice ice ice
ice ice ice ice ice ice ice ice ice ice ice ice
ice ice ice ice ice ice ice ice ice ice ice ice
ice ice ice ice ice ice ice ice ice ice ice ice
ice ice ice ice ice ice ice ice ice ice ice ice
ice ice ice ice ice ice ice ice ice ice ice ice
ice ice ice ice ice ice ice ice

"I knew a girl
Who tried to walk across the lake
'Course it was winter and all this was ice
That's a hell of a thing to do, you know
They say this lake is as big as the Ocean
I wonder if she knew about it?"

ice ice ice ice ice ice ice ice ice ice ice ice
ice ice ice ice (repeat)

y.o. 1981

Cape Clear

In Cape Clear
I saw a little girl crying
She said she lost her teddybear
Oh, then, I can get you another one
No, no, no
It was my teddybear

As we were talking
A cloud passed and cast a pool of light around her
And I saw that she was not a little girl
You are a woman
No, no, no
But you are

All my life I felt like I was in the middle of an ocean
Unable to, unable to touch the horizon
All my life I was floating on my emotion
Not knowin', not knowing life had its own motion

In Cape Clear
I saw a little girl crying

y.o. 1985; song included in *Starpeace*

Video still from *Walking on Thin Ice*, 1981

Video still from *Goodbye Sadness,* 1982

Goodbye Sadness is Ono's elegy to John Lennon through words, music, and images. Using footage from their film collaboration *Imagine,* it commemorates their life together while simultaneously manifesting Ono's sense of loss caused by Lennon's death.

Goodbye Sadness

Goodbye sadness
Goodbye goodbye
I don't need you anymore
I wet my pillow every night
But now I saw the light

Goodbye goodbye sadness
I don't need you anymore
Goodbye goodbye sadness
I can't take it anymore

Goodbye sadness
Goodbye goodbye
I don't need you anymore
I lived in fear every day
But now I'm going my way

Goodbye goodbye sadness
I don't need you anymore
Goodbye goodbye sadness
I can't take it anymore

Hello happiness
Wherever you are
I hope you hear my song
I never want to cry again
Or hold my breath in fear again

Goodbye goodbye sadness
I don't need you anymore
Goodbye goodbye sadness
I can't take it anymore

y.o. 1981; song included in *Season of Glass*

Front cover of *It's Alright,* 1982

It's Alright

Sometimes It's such a drag
I don't feel like getting up in the morning
Then something happens
It clicks in my head
I feel like crying
But I know it's gonna be alright

It's alright, it's alright, it's alright
I know it's gonna be alright

Sometimes, I'm so afraid
I don't feel like facing the world
Then something happens
It clicks in my heart
And I feel like crying
But I know it's gonna be alright

It's alright, it's alright, it's alright
I know it's gonna be alright

I guess I'm not the only one (not the only one in misery)
There many of us around
So when you're feeling down
Hold your heart and say, it's gonna be alright

Hold your heart and it'll be alright. Yes.

I guess I'm not the only one (not the only one in history)
There many of us in history
So when you feel down
Hold your heart and say it's gonna be alright
It's alright, it's alright, it's alright
I know it's gonna be alright

y.o. 1982; song included in It's *Alright*

Never Say Goodbye

Never say goodbye
Never say goodbye
You say tomorrow's another day
All I know is we're here today

I've got nightmares I could never share with you
The kind that keeps me up all night
So hold me tight till the room is light
And tell me that it's alright

Never say goodbye
Never say goodbye
We may go our separate ways someday
But we know we shared our dreams today

I've got nightmares I would never wish on you
The kind that keeps me down all day
So hold me tight till the sky is light
And tell me that it's alright

Never say goodbye
Never say goodbye

y.o. 1982; song included in It's *Alright*

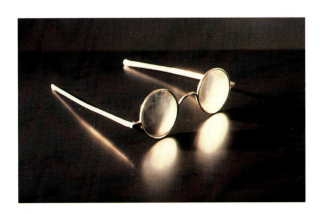

Untitled, (bronze glasses), 1988

BRONZE AGE

Painting to Hammer a Nail In, 1988 (bronze version of 1966 work)

Beginning in 1988, Ono commenced a program of creating bronze versions of a number of her earlier pieces. Doing so dramatically changed the character and the meaning of the originals. In those cases where the original version was in plexiglass, the opacity of bronze resisted the very freedom and effervescence that the earlier material had encouraged. Dreamy intangibility was replaced by the fixed beauty of the bronze patina; mutability gave way to permanence. The two versions reiterated Ono's oft-expressed belief that things can be simultaneously the same and different, that the externals of reality conceal as well as reveal underlying essence.

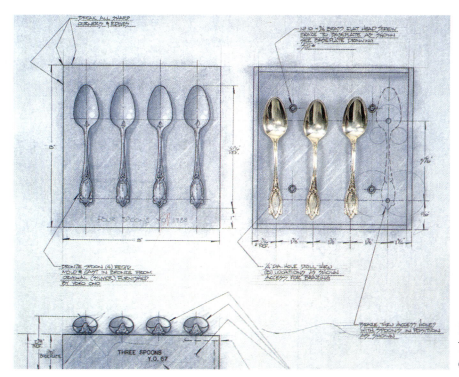

Foundry drawing for Four Spoons, 1988
The Gilbert and Lila Silverman Fluxus Collection Foundation

Bronze Age

During my trip to the Soviet Union to attend a peace conference, I visited the beautifully restored Summer Palace just outside Leningrad. Each room had two photos on the wall side by side—one taken in the czarist period and the other taken just after the room was destroyed by the Nazis. The sepia photos of the palace in its heyday were dreamy; the black and white photos of the rooms after the Nazi destruction had no trace of the dream, and the restored rooms we walked through were brightly colored—maybe a touch too bright—like a rouged, old face. It was a story of change and survival. It was a story of all of us.

One day in New York, soon after the trip, I was eating spaghetti in an Italian restaurant with a friend. The friend casually suggested I do some objects in bronze. The suggestion was so offensive to me that my smile froze and tears ran down my cheek. "This man doesn't know anything about my work," I thought. I realized then that I had an absolute fear of bronze. But why? Then the thought of the sixties flashed in my mind. The air definitely had a special shimmer then. We were breathless from the pride and joy of being alive. I remembered carrying a glass key to open the sky.

I thought I had moved forward right into the eighties and further. But part of me was still holding onto the sixties sky. The eighties is an age of commodity and solidity. We don't hug strangers on the street, and we are also not breathless. When the big boys shake hands at the summit, maybe it's better that they exchange bronze keys rather than glass ones. In my mind, bronze started to have a warm shimmer instead of the dead weight I had associated it with. Bronze is OK, I thought. Eighties is OK. It has to do. One day, I would become a person who could handle bronze with grace and ease.

y.o. New York, 1988

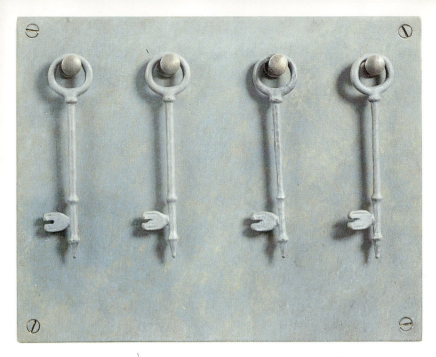
Keys to Open the Skies, 1988 (bronze version of 1967 work)

Painting to Let the Evening Light Go Through, 1988 (bronze version of 1966 work)

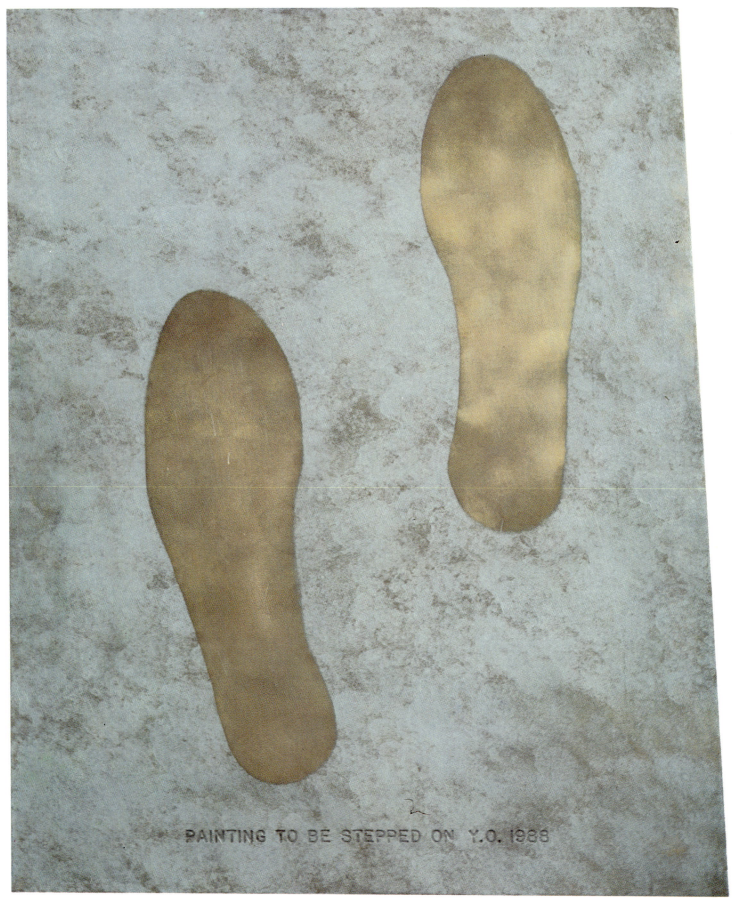

Painting to Be Stepped On II, 1988 (bronze version of 1966 work)

Bastet, 1990

Play It by Trust, 1986–87 (bronze version of Chess Set, 1966)

Play It by Trust, a painted-white bronze version of Ono's earlier piece Chess Set, presaged what would become for her a new foray into bronze. Like a perplexing Zen construct, this piece seemingly denies its own intentionality. Playing chess with pieces purged of their identifying colors was an object-equivalent of Ono's dream of a world without national and ethnic differences. As with Ono's work on behalf of peace, *Play It by Trust* was a symbolic plea for the rejection of nationalism, ambition, and competition.

Bastet

Suddenly one morning, 100 cats landed in my mind. The image was very specific, the posture, the size and the colors. They all had large gleaming phosphorus eyes, came in groups of nine with one on the centerfront, and seemed to be demanding to be materialized. On one hand, I felt like a fool. I regarded myself an intellectual. I was not about to materialize cats as my work. But on the other hand, I thought, wasn't that what I was precisely against—to allow my petty intellectual snobbery block the marvelous flight that art allows us to make? Anyway, to go with the flow and materialize these cats seemed to be the most natural thing to do at the time, and I followed it. I shaped the cats after the one Egyptian cat which looked over the Strawberry Fields permanently from our white room in Dakota.

Then there was a question of what to call them. Usually, I had no difficulty in titling my work since the physical part of the entities seemed to be merely an instrument to enact the concept I expressed in the title. But I didn't know what to call these cats since I only had a vague clue of what they were. It was a totally new game for me. I knew that they were some kind of carriers of a message that descended on us. Should I call them "Transmitters?" That sounded more like parts of electric gadgets. How about "Descendants?" That sounded like a TV soap opera following "Dynasty." Not only I was embarrassed that I could not find a title for them, but I felt worse that I materialized something I didn't know what it was about. Finally, exasperated, I called a friend in New York. "I don't have my Webster Dictionary here. Could you look up some words for these cats? They're some kind of messengers—from far away—I don't know from where though. Could be from Atlantis or something—or from another planet—from way back is what I'm getting." It was interesting that my mind kept playing tricks even at that point. Though I already shaped the cats after the Egyptian cat, somehow I didn't think Egypt, I thought Atlantis. That was my gut feeling: Atlantis or another planet. Five minutes later, my friend called and said that he also did not have a Webster Dictionary at hand and instead he had looked into a theosophical dictionary. A word jumped into his eyes from the first page he opened. The word was BUBABSTE and it was followed with this explanation:

"A city in Egypt which was sacred to the cats, and where was their principal shrine. Many hundreds of thousands of cats were embalmed and buried in the grottoes of Beniassan-el Amar. The cat being a symbol of the moon was sacred to Isis, her goddess. It sees in the dark and its eyes have phosphorescent lustre which frightens the night-birds of evil omen. The cat was also sacred to BAST and thence called (BASTET) the destroyer of the Sun's enemies."

"Oh, dear. If you didn't know that I had materialized the cats before reading this information about BASTET you would think that I had made the cats according to what was said here, wouldn't you?" My friend agreed. So what did this mean? I still wasn't sure. Maybe my mind was not playing tricks after all. Maybe Egypt had something to do with Atlantis and the Space.

The inspiration and materialization of bastet happened in parallel to my initial thought and the performance of hammering nails in a cross in public. On hind sight, I think BASTET may have come to me as my protection. Somehow I know that the two events are connected, that unless I have decided to hammer a nail in the CROSS BASTET would not have come to me.

We would like to thank the following individuals for their assistance in the preparation of *Yoko Ono: Arias and Objects:* Callie Angell, Sam Havidtoy, Jon Hendricks, and Kari Steeves; and Helen Barden, Karla Merrifield, and Dane Worthington of Studio One. We are indebted to them as we are to Yoko Ono, without whose enthusiasm and commitment this project would not have been possible.

    B.H. and J.G.H.

Unless otherwise noted, quoted statements by Yoko Ono were made in interviews conducted with the authors during June and July, 1990.

For the original layouts of Ono's early film and performance scripts, see *Grapefruit*, published by Wunternaum Press, Tokyo in 1964; reprinted by Simon and Schuster, New York, in 1971.

All photographs not credited adjacent to the image are courtesy of Lenono Photo Archive. The following list applies to photographs for which an additional acknowledgement is due.

David Behl: 54, 55, 57-59, 133 (bottom), 134, 136–138; Tony Cox: 46, 47; Fabrizio Garghetti: 26; John D. Drysdale: 99; Nigel Hartnup: 74, 75; Taka Iimura: 80; © Graham Keen: 41; Calvin Kowal: 135; © Iain Macmillan: 18, 19, 40, 42, 43, 56, 61, 68, 76–79, 81-83, 89, 98; Gerard Meola: 130–32; John Prosser: 49; Erich Thomas: 107; Yasuhiro Yoshioka, courtesy of Sogetsu School of Ikebana, Tokyo: 34, 35.